Literacy Goes to School

Literacy Goes to School

the parents' role in young children's literacy learning

Jo Weinberger

P·C·P
Paul Chapman
Publishing Ltd

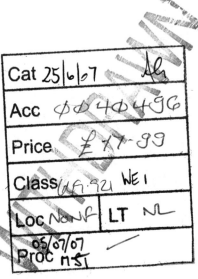
Copyright © Jo Weinberger, 1996

Paul Chapman Publishing Ltd
144 Liverpool Road
London
N1 1LA

British Library Cataloguing-in-Publication Data

Weinberger, Jo
    Literacy Goes to School: Parents' Role in
    Young Children's Literacy Learning
    I. Title
    372.6

    ISBN 1-85396-292-9

Typeset by Dorwyn Ltd, Rowlands Castle, Hants
Printed and bound by Athenaeum Press, Ltd.,
Gateshead, Tyne & Wear.

B C D E F G H 3 2 1 0 9 8

This book is dedicated to
Bob Garber
and to Jake and Matty
with love

Acknowledgements

This book is about parents, children and teachers, and it is to the parents, children and teachers with whom I have worked, who shared their thinking with me, and who helped extend the ideas on which this book is based, that I would especially like to extend my thanks.

I am grateful to colleagues at Sheffield University who have shared ideas and made helpful comments in the process of writing this book. In particular I would like to thank Peter Hannon, Elaine Millard and Cathy Nutbrown.

Bob Garber, my husband, although ill while I was working on the manuscript, followed its progress and was delighted when the book was complete. The book is in many ways a testament to the love, support and encouragement he always gave me throughout his life, which I in turn acknowledge, with love and appreciation.

Contents

Introduction

Dawn is in the supermarket with her two preschool children, Carla and Darryl. Darryl sits in the trolley and points and waves his arms when he sees familiar packaging. He's animated and excited as they pass the tins of baked beans, and again when they go through the cereal section and he spots his current favourite, Frosties. Dawn starts to push the trolley past, but Darryl, who's nearly two, cranes round and reaches out. Dawn takes a few steps backwards, picks up a packet, puts it into Darryl's out-stretched arms, and for a moment he hugs the packet to him, pleased with himself. Meanwhile, Carla, aged three, is helping her mum by fetching some of the items they want from Dawn's shopping list. 'What's next?' Carla demands, throwing a packet of 'Mighty White' sliced bread into the trolley. Dawn looks at the shopping list. 'We need washing-up liquid – you know, the sort we usually have,' and Carla is off towards the lines of bottles, to select the one with the familiar label to go into the shopping trolley . . . On their way home, the three of them call in at the newsagents' to select a birthday card for the children's nanna. On their walk home Carla points excitedly to a 'children crossing' sign which she had noticed earlier in the week on her first visit to nursery. Later in the day they write the card to nanna and both children 'sign' their names, Carla with a big and rather wobbly C, and Darryl with a confident dash of lines across the page. They look in the paper to see when their favourite soap starts, Carla recognising the familiar name in print. While they wait for the pro-gramme to begin, Carla's eye falls on her new book, about the Little Mermaid. She insists that Dawn reads a few pages of it to her, and as she sits and listens, Darryl comes up to see what they're doing, and ends up leaning against his mother, listening too.

This is in fact a compilation of observations of families on a number of different occasions, intended to show some of the many literacy events that are an integral part of ordinary family lives, in which the role of parents, the home and community is central.

Most of it also happens to be 'invisible' when the teacher meets the children and parents at school. When I was a nursery teacher, I was very aware how difficult it was to build up a picture of children within the context of their families. When I had worked as a community worker, and later as a parent myself, I had a sense of how important family context was for children's learning and engagement with school. Against this background, the knowledge I had of children's literacy when they first started in nursery seemed particularly limited, and led me to find out about home literacy across a number of different families, in more depth.

Before we move on to consider what follows in the rest of the book, I want to show you another picture, as a way of illustrating the different literacies of home and school, another key theme of the book. Although I describe the experiences of a teenager, they have direct relevance to the issue of literacy in different contexts.

Imagine a boy of fifteen, Wayne, in the bar of the public house which is his family home, flicking through the *Daily Mirror* to find the sports results. Later, he stocks the back of the counter with crisps, putting the boxes of separate flavours in the places where those working behind the bar will know where to find them. He might have a quick game of darts, writing the initials of the players on the chalk board. All familiar activities with which he feels at ease.

Now see Wayne as I first saw him in the classroom, as his new teacher visiting the class of school leavers who all needed help with basic skills. The students were introduced to me, and one at a time were asked to show me the drawer in which they stored their work. Wayne comes last, awkwardly, reluctant. At the bottom of the drawer is his 'reading book', a Ladybird book from early on in the reading scheme in which Peter and Jane go to the seaside. A card inserted in the book indicates that he has made little progress, indeed he has had the book for a considerable length of time, and has still not managed to complete it. This is not surprising, when you contrast the content suitable for the young child, with which Wayne would have so little incentive to engage, and the adult nature of his life outside the school setting.

This is an extreme example (perhaps it had to be extreme for me to notice it at that early stage in my career), but it certainly left an indelible mark on my perceptions of literacy, and its relevance to different learners in different situations. The image has kept in sharp focus the different expectations of literacy at home and at school. When I worked with very much younger children, this image remained with me, and made me aware of how important it is to have an idea of literacy in children's homes and communities. I have presented these two stories, of Dawn and her children, and of Wayne, to highlight the themes of this book, the central role of parents in young children's literacy development, and the way literacy at home and at school can differ.

The main purpose of this book is to offer you a picture of the nature of literacy practices within a range of families. Some of the families you meet, and the literacy events and practices of their homes, will probably seem very familiar, others may reflect situations that are new to you. The book may put into words for you some of the things that you instinctively know about families, but have never really consciously thought about. Alternatively, some preconceived ideas about children's literacy learning at home may be challenged. I intend to look at the literacy practices of families first of all in their own right, and then in relation to schooling. First of all, then, I want to ask, what do we see? What is the nature of literacy at home rather than school? Secondly, I want to ask what does this mean for teachers? To begin with, the book takes a theoretical look at a range of studies which start to open up the debate on early literacy and the role of parents, and which put this study in context.

I hope to give clear examples of home literacy learning and show their relationship to school literacy. In so doing I explore the similarities and differences of these two literacies, of the home and the school. Few primary teachers have the opportunity to find out in any detail about literacy learning that has taken place at home with parents. The book will help teachers build on their relationships with parents and deepen their understanding about literacy learning outside school. Doing so can directly enhance children's literacy performance in school.

What I do within the book is to reflect the parents' perspective on children's literacy learning. I draw on a study of how over forty parents, from a variety of different backgrounds, contributed to their children's literacy development at home and at school. The views of the parents are reflected in their own words. The findings from the study are then related to classroom practice through practical suggestions of ways in which teachers can assess and develop their own practice in relation to home literacy learning and relations with parents.

It is widely recognised that partnership between parents and teachers is important for children's learning, but most books address this subject only from the school's perspective. Here we look from the perspective of the home. The variety of experiences, across a range of children and families, will show the complexity and extent of home literacy learning.

The book is divided into three distinct sections:

Part One: Parents' contribution to literacy

Part One brings together the relevant literature on the role of parents in children's literacy development. There are wide-ranging references, from this country and abroad, which makes this section a resource for students, and others interested in a theoretical perspective.

Chapter 1 looks at children's acquisition of literacy from an emergent literacy perspective. This view suggests that literacy development starts soon after a child is born. Young children acquire literacy by being surrounded by print, observing people interact with it, and interacting with it themselves, often in the company of more experienced literacy users. Differences between the literacies in the contexts of home and school are introduced.

Chapter 2 is concerned with the role of parents in literacy development, and looks at the research evidence about this. Research in the past has shown that home background is an important factor in literacy development. This chapter looks at research studies that have revealed what children learnt from their parents at home about literacy.

Chapter 3 reviews home–school relations and literacy development. The role of parents as perceived by schools has changed over the years. The trend has been from an idea that parents should be excluded from an educational role, to ways of involving parents, in particular, during the 1970s and 1980s, involvement in the teaching of reading. More recently there have been tentative moves in the direction of recognising what parents are already doing, in an attempt to recognise and build from this base. This chapter examines the move from schools making it clear that there were to be 'No parents beyond this point', to looking at parental involvement in school-initiated learning, and broadening the approach.

Chapter 4 surveys the effects of the parents' contribution to literacy achievement. This chapter will focus on previous research studies which have pointed to relationships between children's early experiences and their later literacy development. The chapter will be particularly useful to those interested in pursuing research in this area, and those wishing to back up their practice with evidence. The topics explored are literacy learned at home, studies of children who read before school, nursery rhymes and phonological awareness, stories and familiarity with books, writing learned before school and parents teaching reading.

Part Two: Literacy development through parents' eyes

Part Two focuses on findings from the Elmswood Study, a research study of over forty parents from different backgrounds, and their views about children's literacy development. The parents' perspective will be illustrated using relevant, short quotations from the parents themselves.[1]

Chapter 5 is concerned with children's literacy at three. I explore what the Elmswood study has to say about children's literacy at home at age three, using a framework outlined in Appendix 1. It covers a wide range of topics: parents' provision of resources and opportunities for literacy, literacy models and parents' interactions with literacy events and practices with their children.

Chapter 6 then looks at children's literacy at seven. Using the same framework as in Chapter 5, I look at what the Elmswood study found about children's literacy at home at age seven.

---

[1] Where children's and parents' names are given, these are of course not the real names of those involved in the study.

Chapter 7 is concerned with home–school relations and literacy. It reviews the relationship of home and school in connection with literacy in the Elmswood study. The issues explored are parents' involvement in children's reading, literacy in school, parents' knowledge of literacy teaching, contact between parents and teachers, encouragement to parents from school, and parent and teacher perceptions of different literacies within the contexts of home and school.

Chapter 8 looks at the factors influencing the parents' role in their children's literacy development. In this chapter I return to the framework for looking at the influence of parents on their children's literacy development (outlined in Appendix 1). It is here that some of the influences affecting parents are explored, including sources of advice, information about literacy, ideas on reading to children, reasons for sharing books, perceived benefits of literacy and parents' expectations of literacy.

Part Three: Implications for early childhood educators

Part Three shows how the early home experiences of children in the Elmswood study directly affected their literacy in school. This leads on to the practical part of the book. Suggestions are made about how to translate the main messages of the book into practice.

Chapter 9 focuses on highlighting the children's favourite books. One of the key findings of the Elmswood study was the impact of favourite books when children were aged three on their later literacy achievements in school. The focus of this chapter is on translating this finding into practical applications for those working with young children and their families. It looks at the role of favourite books, explores issues concerning the books that we do offer children, and discusses ways of increasing access to books.

Chapter 10 looks to extending home–school relations. Another key finding of the Elmswood study was the influence of parents' knowledge of school literacy teaching, and teacher–parent dialogue on children's literacy achievements in school. This chapter offers teachers a practical way of reviewing their current level of contact with parents, and gives ideas of how to instigate and monitor change through use of a Matrix evaluating home–school literacy. The aim here is that through increased teacher–parent dialogue the children's literacy learning can be enhanced.

The book intends to offer balance by providing the opportunity for early childhood educators to add the parents' viewpoint to their existing perspectives on children's literacy development.

Part One: Parents' Contribution to Literacy

1

What is Early Literacy Development?

This chapter provides a theoretical overview of children's early literacy development. It covers key ideas in relation to environmental print, the contribution of rhyme and phonological awareness, reading and the impact of stories, emergent writing, parents as models for literacy and the concept of different literacies.

Emergent literacy

Over the past decade there have been significant changes in ideas about how children become literate. Many of those concerned with early literacy find that an emergent literacy perspective provides a useful explanation of children's literacy development. This model suggests that literacy development starts soon after a child is born. Children learn to become literate by being surrounded by print, by observing people interact with print in a social context, and by interacting with print themselves. Children see images and logos repeated on advertisements, on television, on packaging that finds its way into the home. They may see parents or other adults reading a newspaper or magazine or responding to a note or letter, and they may want to add their name to a card or gift, or pick up a book or comic to look at.

The emergent literacy perspective is concerned with what children can do, and it deliberately builds upon the understanding and knowledge children build up, incrementally, about literacy. Literacy teachers can assume some knowledge of literacy as a starting point because contact with print is an almost inevitable consequence of living in the developed world. In many ways, both overt and subtle, it impinges on our day-to-day lives.

The term 'emergent literacy' is a helpful description in that it includes children as agents in their own learning (some of the literacy learning emerges from a maturing understanding about language which originates within the child), and the fact that literacy learning emerges with increased experience over time (Hall, 1987). Yetta Goodman's (1980) research into young children's behaviour with print led her to conclude that literacy learning is a 'natural' response as children try to make sense of the world around them. She developed the metaphor of different aspects of literacy as 'roots' which can develop simultaneously, and which will feed the 'tree' which is literacy. The 'nutrient' for the roots is the child's environment.

As they learn to read and write effectively, children begin to develop increasing understanding about how print operates. They need to understand, if not articulate, various attributes of the written word, importantly that print represents meaning, through sounds and words, and other aspects, such as that print has directionality. This is learned behaviour, some of which can occur almost imperceptibly as children encounter print as part of their daily lives – for instance, recognising a familiar food package or clothes label while out shopping, having a book read to them at home, or writing their name on a birthday card. Obviously the more encounters with print the children have, with experienced readers on hand to answer questions or point things out, the more likely is their understanding about print to develop.

Environmental print

In many parts of the world, children are surrounded by print from the time they are born. They see lettering on billboards, street and road signs, on food packaging, labels, advertisements on television . . . they see it in their homes, on the street, in shops and clinics . . . the list is endless. Much of this print is transient, and almost literally 'flows' through neighbourhoods and households. Think of the number of free newspapers and other forms of junk mail that find their way through your letterbox, packaging with print on that is temporarily in your possession, shopping lists and memos that have a short life. Do young children pay attention to this print, and if so, what meaning does it have for them? Various studies (for example, Taylor, 1983, Heath, 1983) indicate that preschool children notice this print and that for them it usually has meaning in relation to contexts which they understand and with which they are familiar. In the USA, numerous studies have looked at children's responses to environmental print. Hiebert (1978), for instance, found that children recognised print from its environmental context rather than recognising the words as such. Goodman (Goodman and Altwerger, 1981) also found that children could make appropriate responses to labels on household goods when the context was available, but this declined sharply if the context was removed. Harste, Woodward and Burke (1984) found that when preschool children were asked what the printed words on a variety of packages said, they generalised and said what the item was used for rather than 'reading' the print. The children knew, for example, which packaging should contain toothpaste and which should contain mints. Their 'readings' in terms of the meaning of environmental print were far more accurate than their reading of their own written stories or of published children's books, probably because the environmental print they encountered was so familiar to them. What is most meaningful to children is what message the print is putting across, and this is often of more importance to them than the exact form the words take. The function of the print takes precedence over the form. Advertising is becoming increasingly sophisticated, often designed to be attractive to a broad spectrum of the population, and children now absorb meaning, if not the exact content, from a wide variety of logos and other messages.

A recognition of children's response to environmental print contributes to an understanding of their literacy development. Environmental print is widely accessible, children do notice it and try to make sense of it, and for many children it may be their first meaningful encounter with print. Margaret Clark (1976), found that while some of the children she studied began reading through their interest in stories, many began through interacting with environmental print, such as signs and advertisements. This learning can occur unnoticed by adults, as young children are often able to absorb for themselves messages from print around them. Payton (1984), for instance, who wrote a very readable account of her own daughter's literacy learning, gives an example of her daughter recognising 'Co-op' on a receipt whilst out shopping, without any recollection of her previously asking or being told about what the word said. It is beneficial if adults help children make these meanings by pointing out print and reinforcing the child's growing awareness; interactions with more skilled literacy users will help children to extend their literacy knowledge.

Rhyme and phonological awareness

Many children are fascinated by rhymes, and enjoy using them, in both real and invented words. Like print, rhyme is prevalent in the social context of small children, in the form of nursery rhymes, jingles, songs and slogans. Recently, rhyme has been shown to have a direct link with some aspects of learning to read.

So that they can understand the different sounds made by symbols in our alphabetic system, children need to be able to distinguish separate sounds within the stream of language they hear when people talk and read aloud. Another way of describing this is to talk about children's phonological awareness. There is evidence to suggest that this is helped by a familiarity with nursery rhymes, and other rhymes and jingles, which play with sounds and reinforce rhythm patterns and rhyme. Some children, for whatever reason, seem to be more sensitive to rhyme than others. This facility links directly to the ease with which children learn to decipher print (Bradley and Bryant, 1983, 1985). The work of Goswami and Bryant (1990) has also shown that some aspects of rhyming are strong predictors of later reading ability. Later research explored the connection between children's awareness of rhyme and their knowledge of nursery rhymes (Maclean, Bryant and Bradley, 1987, Bryant *et al.*, 1989) and found a strong relationship between the two. It is likely that the cultural influence of parents (and other significant people) repeating rhymes at home influences preschool children's familiarity with nursery rhymes, and that affects the ease with which children acquire literacy. Rhyme and phonological awareness needs to be fostered in children, as a way of introducing an important aspect of literacy.

Reading

Historically, reading has been seen a passive activity in which the reader decodes written symbols, and finally arrives at meaning. A psycholinguistic model which fits with an emergent literacy perspective suggests that readers actively make meaning and bring to print their prior knowledge of the way language works and some expectations of what a particular text is likely to contain (Goodman, 1973, and Smith, 1978). This model presupposes that learning to read is not a question of learning the prerequisite subskills, which once consolidated, can then be applied to actually reading, but that reading is a holistic process. The primary way to learn to read is by reading. The work of psycholinguists has sometimes been misinterpreted when it is assumed that, because children are seen as active meaning makers who can learn alongside effective literacy users, the 'teacher's' role is redundant. This is not so. It is very important for young children to have an experienced reader to guide and help them in their reading. They need experienced readers to explain their misconceptions and teach them, at appropriate times, about aspects of literacy they have not yet fully understood. Ferreiro and Teberosky (1982) have shown that children will try to make sense of written material presented to them, but they can misinterpret it. They may, for instance, think that the size of an object determines the size of the word that relates to it, so that the word for bear would be bigger than the word for duck. These misunderstandings, arrived at in a logical way, can be modified through help and lessons given by experienced readers, and further experience of the characteristics of the written word.

Part of being able to learn to read effectively is having an understanding of the conventions of book language. Understanding these conventions can only be arrived at through experience with written language. This particular aspect of literacy learning is learned socially and culturally, and is not a form of learning that arises developmentally from within the child . The language in which books are written is often not the same as the way we speak. The text is decontextualised, which is to say that it does not arise directly from the child's own experiences, but has its own logic and internal meanings. Children need to be able to make sense of it in their own right. Once children have had experience of a number of books, they may be able to guess what might happen next, using the context of what has gone before, and how the author might write about it, which helps them to make sense of new texts. Meek (1988) has applied the work of critical theorists to children's reading. She shows us that it is the reader who actively makes the text have meaning for them, through bringing their prior knowledge of life and the way other texts work to the words on the page. Picture book reading has its own special lessons. In the interrelationship of text and picture, children learn to understand the complexities of literary devices such as intertextuality (the subtle references of style and vocabulary to other similar texts) and irony.[2]

However, we also need to bear in mind that narrative is not the only form of continuous text, and many children, especially boys, often respond more readily to non-fiction (Barrs and Pigeon, 1993). Finding facts about topics that interest them can absorb young children, and many publishers are now responding to this with accessible books which combine information texts with appealing illustration. At home, children may read from a different range of resources from those found in school. For example, in a study of preschool children from low-income families more didactic narratives and non-narratives were read at home than were read in the preschool setting (Dickinson *et al.*, 1992).

While not all children own books or are library members, most have at least some access to print with which to gain experience, however modest, of what it is to be a reader. For example, Wells (1987) found that while not all the children in his study owned books themselves, many have had some access to magazines or mail order catalogues which the children spent time looking at.

Stories

Story is an influential form of transmitting culture, and is widely used in early years education, as well as in children's own homes. Stories allow for the exploration of abstract ideas, emotions, life situations and other people's perspectives. The reading and writing of stories are interconnected. As the Kingman Report (1988) suggested,

> As children read more . . . they amass a store of images from half-remembered poems, of lines from plays, of phrases, rhythms and ideas. Such a reception of language allows the individual greater possibilities of production of language.
>
> (DES, 1988, 2.23)

There has been research that has shown that young children's familiarity with story can enhance literacy development at later stages (Wells, 1987, Wade, 1984).

Most children have encountered stories before they start in school. We need to remember that stories can be accessed orally, as well as through

---

[2] A particularly readable account of an author's awareness of the separate lessons of pictures and words, combining to make a complex tale, can be found in Jan Ormerod's account of her reworking of The Story of Chicken Licken in *After Alice* (Styles *et al.* (eds.), 1992).

other media such as television, videos, computer games, film, theatre and pantomime, so that the act of reading, while a very powerful way to engage with stories, is certainly not the only way.

Children may well be told stories by their parents and other significant people in their lives, they will probably encounter stories if they have experience of watching television and videos, and most children will have had some experience of stories in books as well. Stories can provide a powerful way of assimilating culture. Bruner (1987) suggests we have a predisposition to relate to stories and this may explain their pervasiveness,

> Insofar as we account for our own actions and for the human events that occur around us principally in terms of narrative, story, drama, it is conceivable that our sensitivity to narrative provides the major link between our own sense of self and our sense of others in the social world around us.
>
> (Bruner, 1987, p. 94)

We often make sense of our experiences and tell others about ourselves through story, and often through story we learn new ways of looking at and responding to the world. Stories also show children what they might expect to encounter in the world. At first children do not separate fact and fantasy, but the power of stories is that they deal in universal truths that transcend these divisions,

> it is these underlying patterns, not the witches and giants which give them their concrete form, which makes stories an important agent of socialisation.
>
> (Applebee, 1978, pp. 52–3)

Stories are important because they describe different experiences from those children are familiar with, and will take them beyond what Wells (1987) has called the 'naming and rote recall' of other types of reading experiences. This is where children point to and label familiar pictures by name, like 'ball', 'cat', or by attribute such as the sound an animal makes, like 'woof woof', which is a common experience for many small children.

Children's access to story and the conventions surrounding their telling or reading is culturally determined. Heath's influential study of language and literacy learning in three different communities found that the style of story making differed markedly between the communities; the reading of stories was not universal, and featured more regularly within mainstream than non-mainstream culture (Heath, 1983).

Stories convey powerful messages about literacy and socialisation, and are important later for children's acquisition of school-based literacy.

Reading to children

One of the ways in which very young children learn about literacy is by parents reading to them (Baghban, 1984). Through this experience, children can acquire some understanding about literacy, which is an important part of their learning to read and write. Children can begin to see themselves as readers through memorising books, often having favourite texts (Sulzby, 1985). Children who are read to often act like readers themselves (see, for instance, Sulzby and Teale, 1987). There are social class and cultural differences in both how and indeed whether storybooks are read to children (Scollon and Scollon, 1981).

In being read to from the continuous text of books, children have the chance to learn about the decontextualised nature of print. This is something that they cannot acquire from their encounters with environmental print. What the child learns from being read to can be generalised to other encounters with decontextualised text. They also learn about the 'sustained meaning-building organisation of written language and its characteristic rhythms and structures' (Wells, 1987, p. 151).

Book reading is an activity which is often routinised, with the speech used being more complex than that used in many other activities engaged in by parents and children (Snow, Nathan and Perlmann, 1985).

Children can learn a great deal about literacy from having books read to them, with adults providing a 'scaffold', where the adult supports the child's current abilities and provides help for them to move on to the next stage. Children who are read to more frequently at home from a young age show increased interest later, in listening to stories within a nursery or preschool setting (Morrow, 1983). Re-readings of a known text can be particularly fruitful as the child comes to memorise text and story, later being able to read the text for themselves, recreating the text while following the print and pictures on the correct pages. This repeating of favourite texts can give children

> a feeling of mastery as well as a solid familiarity with linguistic forms and a growing understanding that texts can endure and yield more on a second or even third reading.
>
> (Dombey, 1992, p. 15)

Re-reading allows children to 'know the essence of storyness' (Goodman, 1980). When a child has a book read to them it

> provides a child with exposure to more complex, more elaborate and more decontextualised language than almost any other kind of interaction, and the ability to understand and to produce decontextualised language may be the most difficult and most crucial prerequisite to literacy.
>
> (Snow and Ninio, 1986, pp. 118–19)

Thus book reading is not an end in itself. What the child learns can be generalised to other encounters with decontextualised text.

Children who are read to by others can learn that print conveys meaning, that books are read from front to back and print from left to right, that print is made up of letters, words, punctuation marks and spaces, and there is a special language for books and print, for example, 'page', 'word', 'letter'. Children can also learn lessons from having experience of books with several layers of meaning, or 'polysemic texts' (Meek, 1988), so that they begin to be aware of the complexities of written language. It is these various aspects of written texts that children need in order to make sense of a good deal of their early formal schooling, and it is probably for this reason that experience of listening to stories and knowledge about books and print has shown a strong correlation with later reading achievement (Wells, 1985b).

Writing

The emergent writing approach has helped to transform the way in which children's writing is viewed. From this perspective, writing is seen as significantly more than transcription, handwriting and orthographic skills. Researchers have observed the way young children make deliberate marks on paper, which then change with increased experience, and have seen how children behave as authors, actively making meaning. At first their marks may not even approximate conventional writing, but gradually and with encouragement, children move nearer to the written word as we recognise it. Even in the very early stages, children's writing often takes on visual similarities with the script the child is most familiar with. Harste, Burke and Woodward (1982) provide clear examples of differences between English and Arabic speakers in the overall form of young children's writing before conventional letters have been learnt. The children's letter-like marks look completely different from each other as they closely resemble in style those of the conventional adult form. This demonstrates the socio-cultural dimension of writing. For children, learning to write is not only about developing the necessary abstract skills, but also learning to use these skills appropriately, which is determined by the culture in which one lives.

In their writing development, children usually produce scribble initially, or a sequence of lines or circles or dots, or a combination of these.

This is often followed by using letter-like shapes and some conventional letters that are familiar – often the letter that begins the child's own name. These are used in different combinations in order to mean different things (see Figure 1).

Once children begin to understand the relationship between sounds and letters they can use this knowledge to 'invent' spelling for themselves. Read (1971) pointed out that children usually spell in a systematic way. Some errors occur because while the sounds are often represented accurately, the conventions of how we usually write the word have not yet been learned. Children's spelling at this stage is to a large part dependent on their phonological awareness (Goswami and Bryant, 1990). To begin with, children often write in syllables rather than distinct phonemes, and also pay attention to consonants rather than vowels. This pattern of development is not arbitrary, but is based on the development

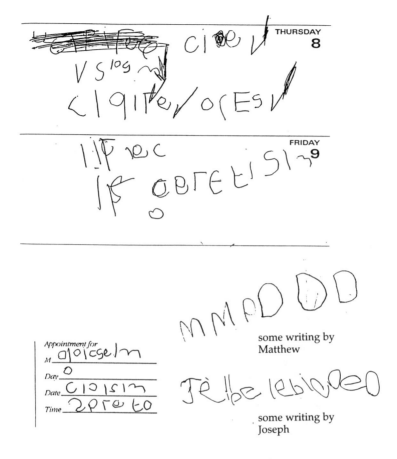

Figure 1   Examples of children using letter-like shapes and some conventional letters

of children's thinking about writing, which is entirely logical (see the examples in Figure 2).

What children need to extend their writing is experience, support and feedback. This gives children the opportunities to construct the rules of writing for themselves. We can see this development when individual children's writing is recorded over time (Bissex, 1980, Schickedanz, 1990). Conflict between the children's view of how things should be written, and writing produced by others, leads them on to further development (Ferreiro and Teberosky, 1982).

Most preschool children are keen to 'write', and if given materials and a context will readily do so. Nigel Hall (1987) showed that when introducing literacy resources into the homecorner at nursery, children were very keen to 'write' in a way appropriate to the setting, for instance, if a pad was placed near a toy telephone, they would use it to record a phone message.

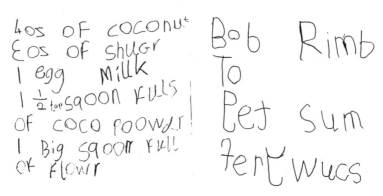

(Bob remember
to
get some
fireworks)

Figure 2   Examples of children's 'invented spelling'

Although children's writing develops at different rates, children may already know many significant features of writing when they first enter school. They may know that it is meaningful, and is to communicate messages, that written language is composed of separate marks, and that the writing has certain forms and structures (Hall, 1987). Writing does not just happen. This experience is gained through interacting with print which has already been produced, and learning from more experienced writers. If young preschool children are writing at home, then their family are probably involved in some way, since it is they who provide the child's context for learning.

Models of literacy users

Vygotsky's work (1962, 1978) has been influential in highlighting the important role of social and cultural context in extending children's learning. The role of the parent is central to the social context of the preschool child. Models of literacy are important for children's literacy development. Parents who read at home and act as a model of what it is to be a reader encourage their children's interest in reading (Nebor, 1986). Some studies of early readers have shown that their parents were often avid readers (Clark, 1976). Parents who enjoyed reading as a leisure activity were more likely to have children with a high interest in literature (Morrow, 1983). Wells (1987) found that the children who were the most accomplished writers by the age of nine and ten, had parents who wrote frequently, often 'lists, memos and notes', forms of writing which were both visible and recognisably purposeful. Another way in which adult models of literacy impact on children is through play. Literacy-related play arises from children's observations of the world around them, and pretend play gives children the chance to explore the social roles that they observe the adults in their world carry out. Since many children are involved in make-believe play with some literacy content before they go to school, this probably arises from experiences observed at home or involving parents. Play which includes some aspect of reading or writing can extend the child's current level of understanding of literacy.

Different literacies

Literacy is not a product, made up of autonomous skills which we learn to become fully literate. It is rather a succession of on-going literacy practices and events which vary according to different situations (Barton, 1994). Literacy practices refer to culturally influenced patterns of using literacy; and literacy events are the occasions on which people actually interpret or create aspects of literacy. Brian Street, an anthropologist, has been influential in recognising and recording this new view of literacy. He talks about the contrast between an 'autonomous' model, and an 'ideological' model of literacy (Street, 1984). The autonomous model tends to be teacher centred, with a focus on specific books and tests, while the ideological model represents a learner-centred approach to literacy. Although the National Curriculum is very specific about the skills children need to acquire to develop their reading, writing, speaking and listening, if we take a broader view of how children actually use literacy, the situation is actually much more complex. We can talk of literacies in the plural, rather than of one single 'literacy', and how these different literacies are associated with different social contexts (or domains) of life. The literacy practices of young children with their parents at home are often different from the literacy practices the children meet in nursery and at school. In school, literacy teaching and learning is largely overt and specific, whereas at home, it often occurs almost invisibly as an integral part of some everyday activities. Tizard and Hughes (1984) and Wells (1987) found that at home the most frequent and often the most fruitful context for literacy learning was in the course of day-to-day family activities. A central purpose of this book is to document these different literacies, to point out their similarities and differences, and to explore the connections between them.

To summarise, what I have described in this chapter is a general view of children's literacy development. Because the development occurs within a cultural and social context, children from different backgrounds will necessarily have different experiences. These experiences will inform the child's developing view of literacy, which usually starts shortly after birth, and certainly well before the child goes to school. Frank Smith (1978) contrasted a naturalistic, incremental view of reading (which for our purposes could equally well be applied to other forms of literacy) with a mechanistic view which makes a clear division between readers and non-readers:

The term 'learning to read' can be misleading, if there is an assumption that there is a magical day in every literate person's life, some kind of threshold, on which we become a reader but before which we are merely learning to read. We begin learning to read the first time we make sense of print, and we learn something about reading every time we read.

(Smith, 1978, p. 128)

If we supplement the term 'to read' with 'to be literate' we arrive at a picture of someone interacting with print, and learning over the course of a lifetime. Learning to be literate is a complex, culturally shaped process.

This chapter has laid the groundwork in mapping out the major attributes of early literacy development. It has given an indication of the understanding about literacy which children in the developed world are able to acquire before encountering formal schooling. In the next chapter we look more closely into the way in which home background influences the ways in which children encounter and interact with literacy practices, showing the centrality of parents and the home for children's literacy development.

2

Home Background and Literacy Development

We saw in Chapter 1 that literacy learning occurs right from the beginning of a child's life, and takes place in the familiar settings of home and community. At the heart of this view of literacy development is that parents and the home play a central role. Looking at other studies provides a way to contextualise the findings from the Elmswood study, which follow in Part Two, and in this chapter we look at studies which suggest a clear relationship between home background and literacy development. Whilst acknowledging that children have their individual predisposition, we need to recognise that much of their literacy learning arises from, and is influenced by, the social environment in which they find themselves. Virtually all children born into a print culture have a great deal of experience with the written word at home and in their communities, often mediated by their parents, before they formally start school.

Children learning in a home context

Many of the literacy events and practices around us are so familiar that we no longer consciously 'see' them. By deliberately drawing them to our attention, we are able to look in a more informed and purposeful way and raise our level of awareness of the aspects of literacy which we are examining. A useful way of describing this process is as a way to 'make the customary visible' (Taylor, 1981).

Some studies have done this for us. In Shirley Brice Heath's *Ways with Words* (1983), for instance, she presents a detailed study of language and literacy in three communities in the Carolinas, Southern United States. In this book we are shown extensive examples of children learning in a home context, and what this means for their literacy development. Heath found different child-rearing practices and ways of engaging with literacy events in three communities: Roadville, a white working class

community; Trackton, a black working class community; and the group Heath refers to as 'townspeople' who were teachers' families living in the town. Through careful observation and analysis Heath highlights continuity and discontinuity between literacy in the different communities and in a school setting.

What she found was that the children of the townspeople tended to be the most successful at school, and it was the townspeople who most often read with their children, talked to them and played with them before school. Once the children went to school, values were in many senses shared between the two settings. The children had had plenty of experience of stories, they had had practice at labelling and naming things, and were able to make up stories about things that were not necessarily present at the time (experience of decontextualised language, so important for school-based learning).

In Roadville, while the parents were keen to prepare their children educationally until the age of about four, once the children were in church nursery school, the parents tended to feel their role was no longer an educational one. For example, before the age of four the parents often read to their children from their books, but this was likely to stop once the child started nursery. The content of their stories tended to be factual, with fantasy being discouraged, since in that community making things up could also be construed as telling lies. Most of the children's books were of nursery rhymes, the alphabet or picturebooks of familiar objects, labelled with short descriptions underneath, rather than more extended texts. The mothers had access to the Bible, but apart from that their reading tended to be limited to occasional magazines or paperback novels, in fact mostly the mothers felt they did not have time for reading.

In contrast again, the community in Trackton had a much more oral culture, with stories being elaborately told and status afforded those who could embellish their story most effectively and entertain the listener. The content was usually about people and events that others were familiar with, so the context would be known and shared. The adults did not tend to read to the children, and the children did not often have books among their possessions, rather the children were more likely to amuse themselves, or to fit in with the adult activities around them, than in the other two settings.

What we are shown, then, is that in both Roadville and Tracton there were significant discontinuities between home and school, including a lack of experience with decontextualised language, which often made literacy learning difficult for the children at school, whereas for the children of the townspeople there was a much closer match between the literacies of home and school.

Another study to show us in detail children's literacy practices in a home context is *Family Literacy* in which Taylor (1983) described the early reading behaviours of children from highly literate middle class homes within a fifty mile radius of New York City. Taylor found that the parents did not deliberately teach their children, in fact, when they did try to do so, they often met with resistance. Learning at home was seen to be a highly contextualised, complex cultural activity in which children learnt for a purpose, for instance, learning to decipher the 'label on the shampoo bottle, the recipe for carrot bread . . .'. These were not disembodied learning activities, but had significance within the child's daily life. Even when the parents deliberately introduced print to their children, the words were 'locked into the context of the situation', rather than being decontextualised. Many of the children were interested in writing and drawing, and they produced considerable amounts of both on a daily basis. There was variety in the literacy practices of the families, with the only activity that all parents mentioned in the context of their children acquiring literacy was reading stories to their children. All the parents also remembered having stories and print around when they were children.

Does anything similar occur within working class homes? Taylor and Dorsey-Gaines (1988) set out to explore this question in the context of black children living in urban poverty in the USA where at least one of the children in the families studied was successfully learning to read and write at home. They found that a characteristic of these homes, which were economically poor, was that the adults were interested in studying, there were always newspapers and sometimes magazines in the apartments, and reading for pleasure was important to the family members. The children were frequently engaged in a variety of reading and writing activities, which were encouraged and valued by the parents. Their study showed that literacy events and practices can flourish successfully in disadvantaged circumstances. Furthermore, when Teale (1986) observed preschool children from Anglo, Black and Mexican American low-income families in San Diego, USA, he records that he also found examples of literacy occurring in all the homes. Children had similar contact with environmental print, although other literacy events and practices varied between the families. In some homes a great deal of literacy activities occurred, in others very little. As Taylor (1983) also noted, the literacy observed was largely socially defined and for the vast majority of the time was engaged in for reasons other than the reading or writing itself. Literacy was most common in connection with what Teale describes as 'daily living routines'; for example, shopping, cooking, paying bills and travelling. This provides a reflection of how highly literate our society is. In all the homes there was paper and something to write with, and in terms of ethnic group, gender, educational level of parents and family structure, Teale concludes there was as much variation within the different groups as between them.

In this country, Minns (1990) studied the literacy experiences of five preschool children from Coventry, from three ethnic backgrounds, Afro-Caribbean, Asian and Anglo. She also found all had experienced literacy events and practices at home, but that these varied in type and in quantity. She shows how each child enters school with a different reading

ned socially and culturally at home. It is particularly import-
ners to be aware of practices within children's homes that do
the literacy practices of schools.

Wh... surveys tell us about home background and literacy

In general, surveys which include investigations of literacy have shown
the importance of the role of parents, albeit to different degrees and in
different ways, to the development of children's literacy.

Davie, Butler and Goldstein, in *From Birth to Seven* (1972), for instance,
using information about children born in one week in 1958, showed a
strong association between social class and a child's reading performance
at seven when they found that a seven-year-old child of an unskilled
manual worker was six times more likely to have a low reading test score,
than that of a child of a professional worker. This study also showed that
the more education parents had had, the more likely it was that their child
would have a higher 'reading age'. They concluded that much of children's learning takes place before or out of school.

Similarly, John and Elizabeth Newson studying seven-year-olds in
their home environments in Nottingham (Newson and Newson, 1977)
found differences in attitude and behaviour between social class groups.
They found that middle class girls read and wrote the most and working
class boys the least. They found that over three-quarters of the parents
helped their seven-year-old child with reading, or had done so in the
past, and that most parental help with writing was concerned with spelling. They also mention that parents recognised the importance of making
resources available, for example, by setting 'the table out and a nice sheet
of paper and sharp pencils – everything to invite him to write'. While the
vast majority of the parents in their study were anxious to offer help and
support, some felt they lacked the necessary expertise.

A number of smaller scale studies have contributed to our understanding of the role of parents and home background in children's literacy
development. Harste, Woodward and Burke (1984), for example, showed
that one of the most important factors in encouraging early literacy learning at home was not just that materials for literacy were available, but that
they were highly accessible. Formal teaching seemed less successful than
more naturalistic activities of parents and children together. Another important factor in early literacy learning they term 'inclusion'. By this they
mean times when the child was integrally involved in what the adults
were doing. This was often by default rather than by design. For instance,
if the parent was to go shopping, to the doctor's, to cook, write letters or
bills, read letters and so on, this often had to be done with the child, or not
get done at all. Farquhar *et al.* (1985), in a survey of the views of parents
and teachers, found that the majority of parents said they helped their
child with reading and writing at home, with many seeing this as part of
their role as a parent. But nearly a third of reception teachers interviewed

considered that few or none of the children's parents would provide adequate back-up at home to academic work in school, and less than a sixth felt they did not have enough information about what happened in the children's homes to make a judgement. Hall *et al.* (1989) surveyed parents of children who attended nursery and reception classes in disadvantaged areas of Manchester. They found that not only did the majority of parents help their children learn to write before school, they also showed a great deal of interest in this. The parents definitely felt they had a role to play in their children's writing development.

In a study which looked at parents' responses to how they viewed literacy, Fitzgerald, Spiegel and Cunningham (1991) interviewed parents of children beginning at kindergarten in the USA, and assessed the parents' literacy level. They divided parents into 'high' and 'low literacy' groups, to see if there were differences in their ideas about how their children learnt about literacy, and the parents' role in the process. While both groups recognised the relevance of everyday materials, like paper, pens and magazines, 'low literacy' parents found instructional materials, such as alphabet blocks and flashcards, equally important. In contrast, the 'high literacy' parents were not in favour of skill orientated materials and activities. Both groups thought it was interacting with literacy materials that was important, not just owning them. Both groups of parents tended to think of literacy development far more in regard to reading than to writing. They characterise 'low literacy' parents' view of literacy as being concerned with 'a bundle of skills', 'school learning' and 'a school game'. In contrast, the 'high literacy' parents saw literacy more as 'cultural practice', 'out-of-school learning', 'shared cognition' and 'apprenticeship'. These differences were important in showing how differently parents with varied perspectives saw their role. Most importantly, however, all the parents felt they had some role in their children's literacy learning.

These studies all point to the substantial role that parents play in supporting their children's literacy development, some feeling clearer about what they were doing, and more supported than others. In general, surveys have been able to show what a powerful influence parents and the home can have on children's literacy development.

Looking closely at individual children

A number of researchers have studied individual children, often their own, which helps us towards a greater understanding of the process of literacy learning within the context of children's own homes. These studies, together, build a body of empirical evidence about what goes on in the otherwise private world of parents and children interacting on literacy practices at home. Butler (1979), for instance, describes the influential role that books played in the early years of her granddaughter, who has Downs Syndrome. She gives details about her responses to books and the knowledge of the world that became accessible to her as a result of very early and continued exposure to books and stories. She continued to have an interest in books, an ability to read, a competence with language, and a level of confidence which might not otherwise have been expected. Other parents also chart their children's progress in literacy. Crago and Crago (1983), for example, wrote a detailed account of their daughter Anna's experience and response to picture books and stories, up to the age of five. Both her parents read a great deal and had many books in the home. She tended to select the books that were read to her, and was a member of the library from the age of two. She was read to regularly at bedtime, and also during the day. On average, she was read to for about half an hour a day, and sometimes for considerably longer. During this time she encountered hundreds of books, and some she gained familiarity with through repeated re-readings. Crago and Crago show how these experiences helped Anna to become a fluent reader from when she was six. Baghban (1984) in the USA, and Payton (1984) in the UK also followed their preschool children's literacy development. Baghban (1984) showed how familiarity with texts, contact with parents (and grandparents) as models, and access to writing materials, facilitated her progress in literacy learning. Payton (1984) followed her daughter's progress to a stage where she began to read and write with independence. Payton considers the parents' role in sharing stories, providing materials and acting as a model when reading and writing for themselves to be vital. As in many of the other studies mentioned, this learning tended to be spontaneous, rather than the parents setting out deliberately to teach aspects of reading and writing. Adams (1990) provides a small-scale case study of her son. She describes some of his activities, which include thirty to forty minutes a day when his parents regularly read to him. She suggests he was typical of other middle class, culturally mainstream children living in the USA. She calculates that by the time he was to start in first grade, her son would have experienced between 1,000 and 1,700 hours of storybook reading with his parents, watching the book while the story was being read. Contrasted with this, the impact that his first grade teacher would be able to make, taking into account all the other children she or he would also be responsible for, could only be limited.

Teachers must therefore rely on the children's preschool learning at home, on which to build their literacy programmes at school. The implication is that all teachers have to do this, whether they are conscious of it or not. How much better to do it consciously, and build on a foundation that is known.

Parents' literacy interactions with their children

Parents' interactions with their children often occur naturally, without parents being consciously aware of their teaching function. As Leichter (1974) comments, many literacy engagements actually occur 'at the margins of awareness'. Theoretical models which explain parents' behaviour can help to make their role more accessible to us.

Vygotsky (1978) developed the concept of the 'zone of proximal development'. This represents the distance between what children can achieve on their own, and what they can do with the help of someone who is more competent then they are. Successful learning can occur when parents support children to engage in activities just a little beyond their current level of development, but within their 'zone of proximal development', so that with help, children are able to achieve a new level of understanding or competence.

Bruner (1975) suggested the concept of 'scaffolding' to describe the help that a more competent person can give to the child. At first they provide a considerable amount of structure and support, but slowly take away the amount of support given as the child becomes competent on their own.

These concepts explain the behaviour of many parents (of course, of teachers too!) when they interact with their child on a learning task, which will include the learning of literacy.

Literacy learning as part of everyday family activity

Studies of children's literacy development at home have shown that this often happens as an integral part of day-to-day life rather than as something separate (Taylor, 1983).

Parents have a formative role, and most parents also clearly see themselves as having a central role in their children's literacy development. The vast majority of parents involve themselves naturally with their child's acquisition of reading and writing skills. The interaction of this role with the school, and the types of literacy which each emphasises, recognises and rewards, is one that is less clear cut, and where anxieties and misunderstandings can occur through lack of shared understandings. This is a theme we will return to.

In this chapter, we have taken a look at the role of parents and the home in children's literacy development. We have seen that parents often engage in interaction with young children's literacy learning, although there is variety in the ways in which they do so. In Chapter 3 we consider the interface of home with school, and reflect on the nature of parent–teacher relations.

3

Home–School Relations

The way that people working in schools look at the parents' role has been changing over the years. From the idea that parents should be excluded from an educational role, there has been a move towards involving parents in educational activities promoted by schools; in particular, during the 1970s and 1980s, focused on the teaching of reading. More recently there have been some moves to recognise what parents already do, and what children have already learnt at home, in an attempt to build on this base in school.

As we saw in Chapter 2, most parents want to be involved in their children's education, and feel they have a role to play, whether or not this is acknowledged by school. Schools are increasingly recognising the parents' educational role.

'No parents beyond this point'

In the past, many parents felt excluded by schools, and received messages, actual or implied, that teaching reading should be left to professionals. This is felt by many parents to this day. Studies going back over twenty years show how parents have often felt excluded from school. For example, Newson and Newson (1977), in a study which reflected the views of parents of seven-year-old children, reported parents' comments that schools seemed to set out to deter parents. One parent in their study, for instance, asked if she helped her child, said,

> Not since going to the school and talking to his teacher. I found out that we were doing the wrong thing, teaching him a different way, you see, so it's best to leave it alone.
>
> (Newson and Newson, 1977, p. 145)

In studies of children who learnt to read before school, some of the parents said they were wary of telling the school about their child's achievements. They even felt they may have put their child at a disadvantage. Durkin (1966), for instance, working in the USA, reported parents' uneasy feelings about their children's early reading, since they inferred that teachers thought this might lead to later problems. Clark (1976) also showed that parents of children who could read early were made to feel rather embarrassed, and so were reluctant to report the children's abilities to the teachers.

Parents are important

It was the Plowden Report (Department of Education and Science, 1967) which gave the first official recognition, in this country, of the potential role that parents could play in their children's schooling. The report suggested that

> One of the essentials for educational advance is a closer partnership between the two parties (i.e. schools and parents) to every child's education.
> (Department of Education and Science, 1967, para 102, p. 37)

Parents were thus seen to have an important role in encouraging their children, and their potential to support the school was seen as beneficial. Schools were, in turn, encouraged to give more information to parents. Subsequently, other government reports, legislation and official documents have recognised the potential benefits of collaboration between teachers and parents to enhance children's learning (although, until more recently, they have avoided suggestions of actual involvement in the curriculum).

In the HMI (1990) report, *The Teaching and Learning of Language and Literacy*, the agenda lies clearly within the school. The report says that

> At the heart of successful home–school partnerships lies understanding by the parents of the school's policy on the teaching of reading and how it is put into practice.
> (HMI, 1990, p. 14)

However, no mention is made of the importance of parents being able to share with teachers the language and literacy learning occuring at home.

Parental involvement in the teaching of reading

Until the 1980s many teachers felt that parents should be dissuaded from working with their children on reading because it could possibly hinder children's progress. This view has changed, and schools have increasingly acknowledged that parents can contribute to their children's reading development. The work of Tizard, Schofield and Hewison (1982) was influential in highlighting the potential benefits of parents listening to their children reading. In their study of top infant to first year junior children in Haringey, who read regularly to their parents from books sent home by their teacher, they clearly showed positive outcomes for the children's reading (measured by reading tests) when compared with a control group, and a group which received additional teacher help in school. This was followed by similar work elsewhere (Griffiths and Hamilton, 1984, Topping and Wolfendale, 1985). The idea of parents hearing their children read was widely disseminated, and often became part of the primary school's repertoire for teaching reading. Hannon (1987) set up a similar scheme, the Belfield Reading Project in Rochdale. Although he did not find any marked improvements in children's reading test performance, there were other areas of improvement, for instance, in children's motivation to read and their enjoyment of reading. In a study of the specific strategies which parents and teachers used in responding to children when hearing them read (Hannon, Jackson and Weinberger, 1986), many similarities were found between what parents and teachers do, which clearly showed that parents can play a useful role. Moreover, there were important differences between parent and teacher sessions which actually favoured reading at home, for example the possibility of spending more time together on reading, and having fewer interruptions than in class. Additional evidence comes from a survey of 3,000 inspection visits to primary schools (HMI, 1990), in which they found that parental support for reading had a positive effect on children's reading. All this suggests that parents involved in school initiated schemes to encourage them to hear their children read will probably improve children's reading development and their motivation. There are certainly no indications that such schemes hinder children's progress. Many parents are enthusiastic about increased involvement. Here are a couple of typical comments from parents who have taken part in school projects to involve them in their children's reading.

> I hadn't a clue how they were taught to read. Now you know. You're not taking the teacher's job off them; but you're given an insight into how they learn and how you can help them.
>
> (Weinberger, 1983, p. 28)

> I think it's great – about time they did more work with parents. I don't like the idea of school work being separated from home all the time.
>
> (Hannon and Jackson, 1987, p. 23)

Many studies of parental involvement in the teaching of reading have focused on families living in disadvantaged circumstances. The interest expressed by these parents helps to challenge the stereotype of uninterested and unmotivated working class families. These studies show that many parents were interested in their children's education, whether they had the opportunity of showing this practically or not, and when asked by the school, were often happy to be involved. In the Belfield Reading Project it was only those parents who were affected by a combination of adverse factors, which included unemployment, chronic ill health, financial difficulties, and lack of reading material in the home, who did not become involved in their children's reading development (Weinberger, Jackson and Hannon, 1986).

How far has the practice of parents helping their children with reading found its way generally into schools? Is there evidence of anything more than token involvement of a few parents? Hannon and Cuckle (1984), for instance, conducted some research into the extent to which schools encouraged parents to hear their children read at home. Of the sixty children they interviewed, nearly half of them read to someone at home, but when it came to taking home school books and reading these at home, only three out of twenty class teachers gave support and advice on this to all the parents, and only two children had taken a school book home and read it to their parents on the previous night. This suggests that the extent of parental involvement may not actually be as widespread as has sometimes been implied. Indeed, it may be that schools work mainly with parents who are already involved in school-like activities with their children. Toomey (1989), for instance, found that schools he studied in disadvantaged areas tended to work only with the few parents who were already confident in their relationship with the school, and who shared a view of schooling which reflected that of the school and teachers. This marginalised even further the 'hard-to-reach', or low contact parents, and reinforced divisions between parents who knew about and supported what happened in schools and those who did not. Toomey asks how parental involvement in school initiated learning can be prioritised to ensure that it is made available to all families. HMI (1990) also found that in some cases the arrangements for children to take books home from school for reading practice were least effective for those children most in need of such support. So when we talk of parental involvement, it is important to look at ways to include *all* parents.

Home–school communication

For teachers to work effectively with parents, there have to be opportunities for dialogue between them, and a key issue when thinking about home–school relations is the nature of the home–school communication. It appears that this is often of a limited nature; for example, at the pre-school level, Hannon and James (1990) found that because of poor communication between home and school about the children's cognitive development, teachers tended to underestimate what the parents were doing relating to literacy at home. Numerous other studies (Tizard, Mortimore and Burchell, 1981, Blatchford, Battle and Mays, 1982) have shown how limited parent–teacher dialogue has been about children's learning. Yet in a study of teacher–parent interaction, Epstein (1988) found that parents welcomed clear communication with teachers about the curriculum and how to help their children at home. She found that effective parent–teacher collaboration depended less on the parents' background, and more on the teachers' own practices on work with parents.

To what extent might parent–teacher contact influence children's literacy development? From evidence from research studies, it seems it can. In the USA, Iverson, Brownlee and Walberg (1981) explored the relationship between teacher–parent contacts and children's gains on standardised reading tests. They studied nearly four hundred underachieving children, all part of a supplementary reading project which emphasised parent–teacher contact. They found that increased teacher–parent contacts were associated with significant gains in reading scores for younger children. Epstein's (1991) study explored whether teacher encouragement of parental involvement had a direct effect on children's reading scores. She found that teacher encouragement of parental involvement contributed indirectly to increases in the children's reading scores over a school year. Similar findings were also reported by Snow *et al.* (1991).

How can effective home–school links be developed? Hughes, Wikeley and Nash (1994) looked at the types of contact between parents of primary school children, and their teachers, during the introduction of the National Curriculum, and how satisfactory the communication between them was. While a variety of methods were used – newsletters, parents' evenings, work from school, social events, talking with teacher and head, information booklets, parent help in the classroom and parents' letters – their overall conclusion was that the parents' needs were not being met. We see a distinction between schools' wishes to involve parents, and the fact that the needs of parents are not really being met.

These studies indicate the potential for increasing communication between parents and teachers.

Broadening the approach

There is another issue to be addressed here. The focus for involvement of parents in the 1980s was reading and school. More recently there has been a wider perspective, to include other aspects of literacy – how learning to write, learning about rhyme and phonological awareness, and about environmental print all have a dynamic and often mutually reinforcing connection with learning to read. Within the teaching profession, the emphasis in initial literacy is changing from starting with the school to starting with the home. Minns (1990), for instance, studied the literacy experiences of five four-year-old children from Afro-Caribbean, Asian and white families in Coventry before they started at the school and later in their first year at school. She found that each child's experience was unique, but all had had many experiences of literacy, which might not have been known to their teachers. Minns suggests that . . . children's learning can be fully understood only within a framework that acknowledges their lives at home and in their communities (Minns, 1990, p. xvi).

Assessment of children's literacy experiences and abilities at nursery and at school can provide ways of starting a dialogue with parents about what children have learnt at home. For instance, the Primary Language Record (Barrs *et al.*, 1989) begins with a discussion between a child's parent(s) and the teacher. Barrs *et al.* suggest this allows a realisation of how much

> children know and how much they are involved in a range of language and literacy-related activities at home and in the community.
>
> (Barrs *et al.*, 1989, p. 13)

What is needed is communication between schools and all of the parents, with a flow of information in both directions, schools valuing the parents' contribution, time (always a precious and limited resource) set aside for time with parents, and training and support for teachers.

If parent–teacher co-operation is to be developed more fully by schools, then teachers need to know more about the ways in which parents of young children are able to, or would like to, interact with school, including opportunities to listen to information about children's literacy learning that takes place at home. This issue is discussed in detail in Part Two of this book.

4

The Effects of Parents' Contributions to Literacy

This chapter focuses on key studies which show relationships between children's early experiences and their later literacy achievement. Not surprisingly, experiences at home with parents are important, since large numbers of young children spend most of their time with their families.

Literacy at home and achievement at school

What processes in their homes have an effect on children's literacy development? There have been a number of studies that have begun to explore this question. Moon and Wells (1979) reported a key study of home influences on children's reading development. (This was part of the Bristol Longitudinal Language Development Research Programme, a project developed over a number of years.) In this study, Moon and Wells followed twenty children over two years to discover the literacy practices and events that parents and children were involved in at home. They found that parents' interest in and attitudes towards literacy learning and provision of resources for literacy were strongly associated with teachers' assessments of children's reading and the children's scores on reading tests. The children's knowledge about books and literacy before school, which was acquired largely through what parents did with children at home, correlated highly with later reading ability. The effect of this influence was to last – they found that the children's reading abilities remained ranked in the same order during the first two years of school. It was the level of parents' encouragement for literacy and their provision of literacy resources that most fully explained differences in children's progress in reading.

In the *Meaning Makers* (1987) (also part of the Bristol Research Programme) Wells focused on language development. However, some of the most interesting findings related specifically to literacy focused activities. He studied thirty-two preschool children, over several years. Looking for factors which were associated with predicting future achievement, Wells found that differences in oral language ability declined in importance once the children reached school age, but what was most significant were children's abilities associated with written language (reading in particular, but also writing).

The best predictor of overall achievement at seven was a test of children's knowledge of literacy. The children who scored highly on this test tended to have parents who read more, owned more books, and read more often with their children. Wells (1985a) suggested that children's understanding of what he terms the 'mechanics' of written language is a by-product of a deeper understanding about the fundamental attributes of written language which the children had acquired through experience with books at home. The extent of this understanding varied between children, often due to different experiences. By way of illustration, Wells contrasted the number of stories read to two children from the study. One of the children had at least four stories read to them every day while the other had none at all. So the first child would probably have had some 6,000 story-reading experiences by the age of five, compared with none for the second child. Wells's work shows that children with limited preschool literacy experiences had less understanding about the purposes of literacy, or how to derive meaning from print, than their peers, and that made a difference once the children went to school. His work shows that the more children know, with help from their parents and families from the outset, the more able they are to assimilate the lessons their teachers can provide.

Tizard et al. (1988) (who studied children from inner London, many from disadvantaged homes and communities) found that the strongest predictor for reading at the end of infants school was the children's ability to identify letters when they were nearly five years old. What was this related to? Children do not learn about letters in a vacuum. When the researchers looked at the literacy practices of parents at home and how this affected the children's reading and writing, they found that children whose parents provided more exposure to print (through supplying books and reading them to the children) and who had the most positive attitude towards helping the children at home, scored more highly on the tests of reading and writing than others. Snow et al. (1991) also explored the effects of different experiences at home and at school on the literacy achievements of children from low-income families in the USA. Snow and her co-workers studied thirty children over the course of two years. They found that the most powerful predictors of word recognition and vocabulary were the literacy environments of the homes, and the mother's expectations for her child. Home variables explained much more of the variance in children's literacy test scores than did school variables. Five years after the study began, they collected follow-up data on the children's literacy. Although the children had not maintained the rate of progress they had previously made on their literacy assessments,

previous provision of literacy at home was still the most powerful predictor of literacy achievement. This provision of literacy was based on
observer ratings of parents buying books, reading to their children, taking
them to the library and discussing books, magazines and newspaper
articles with them. It was related four years later to word recognition,
vocabulary, reading comprehension, and to a lesser extent, writing. The
second most powerful predictor was the mother's expectations for her
child's education.

In summary, the literacy developed or introduced by parents in the
home has a direct bearing on later literacy achievement. Processes which
are important are:

- the availability of literacy materials at home;
- parents creating literacy learning opportunities outside the home;
- parental encouragement of literacy;
- parental expectations of their child and child's schooling;
- frequency with which parents read with their children and taught them
  about literacy;
- parental contact with school and knowledge about school;
- frequency of library visits;
- extent of book ownership and the variety of print materials in the
  home;
- the literacy environment generally of the home and parents reading
  themselves;
- the child's knowledge of letters preschool;
- the frequency of storytelling at home.

In addition, aspects of the homes which were shown to be relevant to
children's literacy development were:

- social class;
- parents' educational level;
- family income.

Children who read before school

What do studies of early readers have to tell us about literacy development? There have been a number of studies from the 1940s onwards
which have described the achievements of children who began to read
early. Taken together, these amount to a body of empirical evidence
which indicate characteristics that children who learn to read early have
in common with one another. Parental levels of education and social class
do not necessarily make early reading more likely. Most parents of early
readers were keen readers themselves. The parents (and also older siblings) answered children's questions about print when the children asked
– but in a casual, rather than a didactic way. The children had plenty of
access to reading materials especially story books, and often used the

library, and also had access to paper and pencil which they used frequently. Being read to, often with the child on the parent's lap, was a common experience of these children (see Teale, 1978, Baghban, 1984). As well as the children's own motivation, the most striking feature was an interest and engagement in reading events and practices by parents interacting with their children.

Durkin was one of the first researchers to document the significance of early reading for children's subsequent literacy competence. She described characteristics of nearly fifty children from a multi-racial group in California who learned to read early at home. All their families had a high regard for reading and the children had all been read to regularly (Durkin, 1961). She then looked at families in California together with families in New York, where the children also learned to read early (Durkin, 1966). She monitored the children's progress for three years and found their reading achievements were usually better than comparatively bright children who did not begin to read until first grade. The parents of early readers were more prepared than others to give their children help, and were less likely to believe reading could only be taught by a trained professional. The parents spent time with their children, read to them and provided help when asked. They also used books themselves. Durkin did not find a connection between early reading and the socio-economic status of the families. She speculates that this was perhaps because of working in two different geographical areas, or perhaps because in the years between the two studies ideas were changing about when it was appropriate for children to begin reading. She concluded that the mothers seemed to have played a key role in helping their children become early readers, by the provision of materials, acting as a role model, giving their children time and feeling comfortable as an educator of their own children.

Following the work of Durkin, Clark (1976) studied precocious readers in a longitudinal study of thirty-two children in Scotland who could read before they went to school. She interviewed parents from a variety of backgrounds, and found that all of the parents valued education and that the children had had plenty of adult attention. Most of the mothers were free to be with their children for much of the day and read widely themselves, although only nine of the thirty-two mothers had read books about reading, and of those, most were themselves teachers. The children were encouraged to choose a range of books for themselves, and were taken to the library regularly. While the parents had provided an environment for their children conducive to reading, few of the parents had consciously taught their child to read. The parents' help was 'casual rather than systematic', and formed 'part of their daily life rather than something separate' (Clark, 1976, p. 53).

Anbar (1986) was also interested in those children who learned to read early. She interviewed parents of six preschool children from middle class homes, who had learned to read at home in the United States. She suggests that the parents' role was crucial. The parents had interacted with their children on reading-related activities from when their children were very young. They used a variety of methods, such as pointing out environmental print when out together, reading books to their children, making up rhymes and trying to make what they did appropriate and of interest to their child. However, she found that the parents did not set out with the intention of deliberately teaching their children to read.

Background characteristics, or processes within the home, which many early readers have in common include:

- being read to from a young age, together with opportunities to look at a range of books and other printed material at home;
- parents acting as literacy models and being happy to instruct;
- parental help and encouragement of their children's literacy, or even informal help with learning;
- parents' valuing education, parents providing plenty of adult attention;
- children taken to the library and encouraged to choose books for themselves;
- parents interacting with children on literacy-related events and practices from a very young age, not only by sharing books and stories, but by pointing out print and making up rhymes.

Aspects of the homes in these studies included:

- higher socio-economic status;
- better educated parents;
- smaller families;
- larger number of books in the home;
- having an older sibling who read to the child occasionally.

Taken together, all these different research studies show that a home environment that was supportive of literacy learning was an important dimension for early readers.

Knowledge of letters and reading

As well as studies which have shown the value of practices in the home which contribute to children's literacy development, several studies have looked in detail at what children themselves bring to the process. These have reported high levels of association between a knowledge of letters and successful early reading (Chall, 1967, Muehl and DiNello, 1976). Ehri (1983) suggests that the connection is because letter-name knowledge provides the starting point for understanding our alphabetic system, where learners have to identify individual letters, and then process them for sounds. Those children who know some letter-names have already begun to make these associations. Ehri describes a study in which it was no problem teaching letter-sound associations to kindergarten children who could name eight letters, but it was impossible to teach this to children who could not name these eight letters. She suggests that being able to link letter-sounds to letter-names is much easier for children than learning letter-sound correspondences from scratch. Knowing the names of letters so well that the child can respond to them automatically may also be important. Ehri (1983) suggests that either letter-sound or letter-name correspondences could be taught, because the main learning task is to associate a name or sound with a letter shape, not to extract the sound from the name after the name has been acquired.

Many children who had acquired a knowledge of letters before they started school had not been taught systematically, but gained this information incidentally through other interactions with print and literacy events and practices.

Nursery rhymes and phonological awareness

A number of studies have uncovered the importance of phonological awareness for reading development. The better children are at reading, the more sensitive they tend to be to the constituent sounds of a word (Goswami and Bryant, 1990). Conversely, children who have difficulties reading are often unable to differentiate between the different sounds that go to make up words.

There are three ways of separating the sounds within words, all of which constitute a type of phonological awareness. One is the *syllable*, such as 'hol-i-day' (three syllables), which many children are able to recognise. Another is the *phoneme*, which is 'the smallest unit of sound that can change the meaning of a word'. An example would be 'c' as in 'cat', which could, with the change of just one phoneme, become a different word, such as 'mat'. Phonemes tend to be difficult for children to detect in the early stages of learning to read. The third type of sound within words is the *intra-syllabic unit*. This is a unit of sound which lies between the syllable and the phoneme. The sound at the beginning is known as 'the onset', and the sound at the end is known as 'the rime', for example, str-ing, where 'str' is the onset, and 'ing' the rime. The rime often rhymes, so string will share the same ending sound with other words ending in -ing, such as bring, wing, sing. Children will be used to hearing these patterns in nursery rhymes, advertising jingles, songs, and will often play with words themselves, reproducing real and nonsense rimes (Dowker, 1989). Goswami and Bryant (1990) show that children acquire an awareness of onset and rime, and of phonemes, at different stages of development, and many children can detect onset and rime well before they can read. This makes sense in terms of observations of young children's natural interest in rhyme and alliteration. It is through an awareness of onset and rime that children learning to read can start to make analogies between words that share the same onset or rime, and in this way, learn a useful strategy for reading and also for attempting to spell new words (Goswami, 1990). This ability to split phonemes is highly predictive of later reading achievement (Share *et al.*, 1984). Children often start to recognise *phonemes* as a result of learning to read and write using an alphabetic script. However, children's sensitivity to rhyme may also help with the growth of sensitivity to phonemes (Goswami and Bryant, 1990), and so nursery rhymes and other familiar rhymes repeated from an early age at home can make a contribution to children's literacy development. Bryant *et al.* (1989) reported specifically on children's knowledge of nursery rhymes and their later reading achievement. They found a strong relationship between early knowledge of nursery rhymes and success in reading and spelling, after differences in social class, educational level of parents, IQ, and children's phonological skills had been controlled. Their hypothesis was that nursery rhymes make children more sensitive to phonological differences in sounds, and this helps with their reading. The link between rhyme and speech segmentation is that once a child is sensitive to rhyme and alliteration through familiarity with nursery rhymes, they are in a position to hear when words share a common sound, for example, Jill and hill, in 'Jack and Jill went up the hill'. The children can then transfer this sensitivity to the business of reading.

It is most often with parents that children learn and repeat their first nursery rhymes. As Maclean, Bryant and Bradley (1987) point out, 'Nursery rhymes are one example of the informal way in which parents, for the most part unwittingly, draw their children's attention to the fact that words have separable component sounds'.

These studies demonstrate that there is a relationship between phonological awareness, knowledge of nursery rhymes, and children's subsequent reading achievement, and by implication, show the role many parents have in helping children with literacy through repeating nursery rhymes together in the familiar context of the home.

Impact of stories and access to books

What do we know about the relationship between parents reading stories to their children and reading achievement in school? This was something investigated by Walker and Kuerbitz (1979). Parents of elementary school children were asked about how often they had shared stories with their preschool child and their child's response. While parents of all children said they had read to the children at least once a week, some had been read to every day. The children's reading achievement increased with increased frequency of story-time experiences. As well as being read to, these also included children's enjoyment of listening to the stories, requesting stories, and talking with the parent, with the story as a focus. Reading stories with parents before school was a positive factor in successful reading in the early years at school.

Wells (1985b) concluded from his study of children's language learning that sharing stories was the most powerful predictor of later reading achievement. More generally, growing up in a literate environment, where reading and writing activities occurred every day, gave children a distinct advantage for the start of their compulsory schooling.

What influence does being read to from books have on children's literacy development? An exploratory study into the previous experiences of failing readers involved finding out if high school students with reading difficulties recalled having been read to by their parents (Rossman, 1975). Half the students said their parents never read to them at all. Only just over forty of them could remember anything appropriate being read to them at the preschool stage. It was those students who could name a book that they had enjoyed reading recently who all said they could remember their parents reading to them as a child.

Several studies have shown a positive relationship between books in the home (either owned, or ready access through the library) and children's reading ability (for example, Durkin, 1966, Clark, 1976). In terms of reading to children, Sutton's (1964) study suggests that earlier readers were read to from one year or eighteen months, and Feitelson and Goldstein's (1986) study showed that children in 'school-orientated families' were read to from a significantly earlier age than children from 'non school-orientated families'.

Wade (1984) conducted an experimental study to see whether increasing parental involvement in reading stories and listening to their children's own stories would improve children's abilities in 'storying', defined by Wade as 'the shaping and ordering into narrative from personal experience or from fiction' (Wade, 1984, p. 11). The importance of this for the learning process is that learners need to be able to put new learning into their own words, so that it can make sense to themselves. Just over forty children from differing backgrounds were allocated to a control group and an experimental group in schools in the Midlands. Parents of children in the experimental group were given a leaflet explaining the importance of story, and encouraging them to read and tell stories to their children, and to listen to the children tell their own stories. The experimental group produced significantly better results than the control group. A follow-up enquiry eighteen months after the end of the study showed that parents of children in the experimental group read and told their children more stories, during longer sessions, than parents in the control group. In a later study in the USA, Jana Mason (1992) concluded that preschool children learn about how to read by listening to, and talking about, stories with adults. For many children this experience would be with their parents at home. Some children memorise familiar texts, and from understanding the meaning can move towards an analysis of print and word recognition skills.

In summary, these research studies have shown that familiarity with books and stories has a direct impact on children's later reading abilities.

Writing

There have been fewer research studies examining the relationship between writing and children's later literacy development. Kroll (1983) explored the relationship of children's preschool experiences at home to their later writing development at nine. He found that oral language measures did not strongly correlate with later writing ability and nor did parental feedback concerned with oral language. But parental interest in literacy and the child's knowledge of literacy at the preschool level were both highly predictive of later writing attainment.

Blatchford (1991), using data from the study of inner-city London children reported earlier (Tizard *et al.*, 1988), found that letter identification at school entry was the strongest predictor of reading at age seven. The analyses also showed that vocabulary and handwriting skills at school entry were independently related to later reading. Blatchford *et al.* (1985) and Tizard *et al.* (1988) showed that parental help with writing at the preschool stage was related to children's handwriting at school entry. Almost half the parents had taught their children to write their name and other words, and 40 per cent just taught the child's name. Very few parents only rarely taught their child to write, or said they did not do so at all. The study showed wide differences between children in their knowledge about writing at school entry. Children with greater knowledge when they started school, tended to have higher writing scores at seven. Blatchford suggests that even if only handwriting skills were assessed at the preschool stage, these would give an indication of some level of awareness of written language, and that this is related to achievement in writing later. What children knew about writing when they started school was related to help from parents at home. Often schools have worried that parental help might be inappropriate but these results suggest that parental help with writing at home should be encouraged.

Family organisation, relationships and external pressures can also affect children's writing (Snow *et al.*, 1991). Writing, of all literacy skills, is most affected by a child's confidence, initiative and organisational capacity. Writing involves self-disclosure, and therefore makes the writer vulnerable to criticism. Children can gain confidence in themselves as writers when they are encouraged to concentrate on the content of what they write rather than presentation (see Graves, 1982).

While the number of studies looking specifically at the predictive relationship between home variables and children's writing are limited, those factors found to relate to later writing achievement are of interest. They include:

- the parents' interest in literacy;
- the child's knowledge of literacy preschool;
- family reactions to one another and the outside world;
- children's handwriting at school entry;
- parents' help with writing preschool.

These general findings from a range of research studies indicate that parents within a home context have a significant role to play in children's writing development.

Environmental print

Numerous studies show that young readers are responsive to environmental print (for example, Goodall, 1984 and Kontos, 1986). Of course many young children are only able to recognise signs and labels in context (Masonheimer, Drum and Ehri, 1984). To date, however, there have not been any studies which show what effect reading environmental print has for later literacy development.

Make-believe play reflecting adult literate behaviour

Does make-believe play predict later literacy development? Pellegrini *et al.* (1991) found that children's use of symbolic play predicted their emergent writing. They explain the link between symbolic play and emergent writing with reference to Vygotsky's (1978) conceptualisation of writing as a developmental process from play, to drawing, to scribbling, and then to writing. Play and writing both use signifiers to convey meaning, rather than the literal object itself. Isenberg and Jacob (1983) make the same point in their review of literacy and symbolic play when they suggest that it is the process of transforming oneself or objects into something else while engaged in make-believe play that is related to literacy development. Play allows children to practise what they have experienced, including their experiences of literacy. When children are provided with literacy-related resources, it allows them to show what they already know about literacy, and the way adults use it; for example, reading the newspaper, or taking phone messages. Through observations of their parents and other significant people at home using literacy, children build up a picture of what it is to be literate, and how to respond within a print environment (Hall, 1991).

Parents' role in hearing children read

Studies of parental involvement in the teaching of reading certainly do not show that the parents' help with reading and writing at home in any way *hinders* the children's progress in school. It is still popularly believed by some parents and teachers, that parents can make the child's learning to read and write at school confusing by actively helping in the early stages. *It is important to emphasise that there is no research evidence that has shown this to be the case.*

Hewison and Tizard (1980) broke new ground in their work in this area. They investigated what aspects of parents' day-to-day activities with their child had the greatest impact on reading attainment and found that while very few parents had consulted the school about helping their child with reading, and none said the school encouraged them to do this, half the parents actually helped their child with reading. They concluded that parental help with reading had a significant impact on reading attainment. In developing this work, Tizard, Schofield and Hewison (1982) conducted an experimental study in inner London, the Haringey Project, to test the hypothesis that increasing parental involvement in hearing children read at home would increase children's performance on standardised reading tests. Teachers of children at the start of their last year of infant school sent school books home regularly, for children to read to their parents at home. Parallel classes in the same school acted as a control. A further two classes, in different schools, were given extra help with reading within school. The intervention lasted for three years, resulting in significant improvements by children reading to parents at home, but no comparable improvement for the children given extra help with reading at school.

In contrast, Ashton and Jackson (1986), in a one-year parental involvement project in a class of seven- and eight-year-olds, found the intervention produced no significant effect on reading test scores. Similarly, the Belfield Reading Project (Hannon, 1987), which investigated the effects of parental involvement on children's reading test performance, found no significant effect for children in the project. The project, which involved all children from one school with a working class catchment area taking reading books home and reading to their parents every day, gave support for parents through meetings, handouts, parent–teacher contacts and home visits. When reading test results were compared with scores from children who had attended the school prior to the project the differences in test scores between the two groups were small and statistically insignificant.

In their study of children in inner-city London, Tizard *et al.* (1988) found that what was significant for children's literacy development was the number of contacts parents had with the school, and their knowledge about what happened in school. The number of times parents listened to their child read at home did not seem to affect progress with reading or writing. This may be because of the lack of variation, since over 90 per cent of the parents in this study said they heard their child read at least three times a week at some stage during their time in infants school.

The contradictory nature of the findings from these different studies suggests a need for more research into schemes to involve parents in the teaching of reading. Hannon (1987), using evidence from the Belfield project and comparing it with results from the Haringey Project, suggests that such schemes may be most successful with fairly intensive home visiting with children for whom English is a second language, or where perhaps there is limited involvement of the school with parents to begin with. Tizard *et al.* (1988) also suggest merely sending reading books home may be insufficient to raise standards of children's reading, where home–

school liaison is needed to make this effective. Nevertheless, in all the studies it was the children who read at home most frequently who tended to have the highest scores on standardised reading tests. In this way, we can see the benefit of parents' support in hearing their children read.

What does the weight of all this evidence mean? Good primary practitioners put the child at the centre of the learning process. But most teachers actually know very little about the children they teach in their home context. By finding out a little more, teachers would be in a better position more fully to understand the children they teach, and recognise those aspects of literacy the children have already learnt, and those of which the children have no experience. By looking more fully at literacy events and practices at home, teachers would be in a better position to understand children who have problems with school literacy.

In the Elmswood Study that follows in Part Two, I have built upon the findings of the previous studies. Some of the findings are similar to those explored here already. Other factors have come to light that have not previously been fully explored, but which I believe have a significant part to play in explaining children's literacy development, in relation to literacy events and practices at home with their parents. Of course this is important in its own right and is often independent of school. However, from a teachers' perspective, it is also important to look at home literacy learning in relation to children's literacy learning and achievements in school.

Part Two: Literacy Development Through Parent's Eyes

5

Literacy at Home: Children Aged Three

We have seen that children generally learn an enormous amount about literacy in their early years at home, and that literacies vary according to different social contexts. The literacy practices and events children experience at home are often *different* from those which they will experience in school, and often more varied, including more experiences of what might be considered reading and writing intended for adults, but from which children can learn useful social and cultural lessons about what it means to be a reader and writer in our society.

For a minority of children, however, early literacy experiences are extremely limited, and this can make the sorts of literacy events and practices they encounter at school initially very puzzling. They do not know what is expected of them, and have not had the chance to build up a repertoire of appropriate responses to literacy that many of their peers have been able to. I will return to the practical implications of this in Part Three of the book. For now, I turn to the Elmswood Study itself (background details can be found in Appendix 2).

Daily life and literacy practices

The Elmswood Study is an investigation of children's literacy experiences and achievements from preschool until the age of seven. I visited all sixty families who were part of the study at home, when the children were aged three, to talk with their parents in some detail about literacy at home. This was usually the child's mother, but in some cases their father was there as well. I was welcomed in, and found parents more than willing to talk about their child's experiences of literacy.

In presenting the Elmswood Study, I use the Framework (outlined in Appendix 1) of parents providing *resources and opportunities*, acting as *literacy models*, and *interacting with their children* on literacy practices and events. This chapter presents children's literacy as the parents saw and reported it, so it reflects what was happening in the home through the parents' eyes.

Parents provide resources and opportunities for literacy

The range of resources for literacy varied considerably between families, but it is worth emphasising that reading and writing materials were available to children in *all* the families. There was variation within the social class groupings as well as between them.

Print at home

> 'She likes to look at Robin's comics. She likes to look through anything. Even if it's only writing, she'll still look through it.'

Before we look at what was made available specifically for children to read at home, I want to look at the print environment generally. Children are often avid consumers of print, able to make sense of a range of printed matter, as well as material especially designed for them. For example, most of the children looked through mail order catalogues, a very popular activity, and many read other 'adult' items; for example, magazines, newspapers, dictionaries, Bible and prayer books, and trade magazines. In all, the range of printed materials to which the children in the Elmswood Study had access was extensive, and reflected the amount of print that often enters the majority of homes within an advanced Western society, bidden or unbidden. Even when members of the family did not actually purchase any literacy materials, junk mail, advertisements, free newspapers, packaging and other ephemera laden with print made their way into all the homes on a regular basis.

Children's books at home

Almost all the children had some access to children's books at home, and the idea of having children's books around had been taken as a matter of course in all but one family. Even in this family children's books were used, although it was a new departure. The mother, Jane, who herself found reading difficult, had bought three Ladybird books when Kirsty was three. Kirsty's health visitor who had noticed that Kirsty's language development was slow had advised Jane to share the reading of books with her daughter. (Kirsty also liked to look through the *News of the World* Sunday colour supplement that the family took regularly, so other written material would have been available for her at home even though her mother had not at first thought of introducing books.)

About a quarter of the children borrowed books from the local library, and these children often borrowed library books frequently. However, most children (almost three-quarters of them) did not borrow library books at all. Already this shows a wide difference in the number and variety of children's books being introduced into the homes.

Both the quantity and choice of children's books that the children had access to at home varied widely. There were two children who owned no

Figure 3   Types of print in the children's homes

books at all, while James, a child from a middle class home, owned '200 books at least', and was also a member of the local library. You can see the variation in the number of books the children owned, and how many children were library members, in Table 1.

What the table shows is that most children owned between a dozen and fifty books. Those children who owned the least number of books were also the least likely to borrow them from the library. Of the children who owned less than a dozen books each, only two used the library. However, it was very rare for the children to own no books at all, and in these cases it was due to exceptional circumstances. There were only two children who did not own any books at all at the time of interview, and both had recently, and hastily, moved away from difficult domestic situations and had not yet become fully established in their new homes. So, for only a small proportion of the children was access to books constrained, but in these cases their experiences with books were very limited, compared with other children of the same age.

Table 1   Book ownership and library membership of children aged three

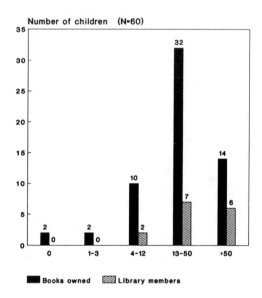

Number of children   (N=60)

Books owned   Library members

Favourite books

As a way of gauging children's level of experience and interest, parents were asked whether their child currently had any favourite books, which they read or looked at often, and which were familiar to them. Many of them said yes. These books tended to give a different view of children's books from those within an institutional setting. When looking at the titles of these books, only eight of the books were ones that one would be likely to find in a nursery setting (see Figure 4). One was a book Mathew had been introduced to at playgroup, *Titch*, by Pat Hutchins. Other fiction books were *The Tiger who Came to Tea* by Judith Kerr (a favourite for Carole and Sarah), *Five Minutes Peace* by Jill Murphy (Rachael's favourite), *The Snowman* by Raymond Briggs, where the illustrations appear without words in a narrative sequence (Thomas's favourite) and *Where's Spot?* by Eric Hill (Samantha and Michael's favourite).

Gordon Wells (1985b) talks of the 'characteristic narrative structures' of story books. Through their choice of favourite books, some of these children were gaining experience of the 'characteristic narrative structures' of the sorts of story books they would later encounter in the institutional settings of nursery and school. Other children were not presented with regular opportunities to gain this experience.

The other favourite books mentioned that one might find in nursery or school were non-fiction, one about sharks and whales and one about dinosaurs. These were favourites for Tim and Barry, and I point out in passing that no girls were mentioned as having a non-fiction book as a

Figure 4   Some of the children's books at age three

favourite at this stage. Most of these children were from middle class homes, only Barry and Mathew were not. There is often a closer match between texts available in middle class homes and school, compared with working class homes and school.

Most of the children's favourite books were story books. There were three children who had nursery rhyme books as favourites, and Rick and Caroline had 'labelling' books as favourites, both Ladybird books, called *My First Big Book* and *All about Me*, which had large pictures and the words printed underneath. Books like these can help children with the acquisition of vocabulary and in answering 'display' questions, of the type, 'what's that?' to which there is a closed response, 'it's a . . . ball, dog, etc.'. This can give parents and children clear roles when looking at a text together, which is an important feature of early language acquisition (Ninio and Bruner, 1978, Heath, 1983). But sharing text at this level becomes restricting in the long term, because children need to move beyond naming to follow more complex narrative and expository written language, so that they can interpret many of the more complex texts they will encounter (if they are to become independent readers) and to meet the requirements of later schooling.

Children's own books

As for books the children owned in general, at least half the parents mentioned those published by Ladybird books, a publishing house with an extensive range of books for children at competitive prices that are widely distributed. Steedman (1982) had also found that Ladybird books were the 'most familiar non-school books' for the children in her study. In the Elmswood study Ladybird books were readily available to the families in the local shops including the post office and the nearest supermarket, and were possibly the most easy to obtain of all books for young children. Many of the books featured characters and stories from series on television. The most often mentioned books by title were those about Thomas the Tank Engine. At the time of the interviews, there was a series of Thomas programmes on television, and the stories and logo were being extensively marketed. Books about other characters familiar on television were also mentioned, for example, Postman Pat, Mr Men, Shoe People, He-Man and Thundercats. Many of these could be characterised as 'ephemeral' in that their themes or protagonists were extremely popular for a time, but then their place was taken by other, similar, books. A few years after these interviews, I went to look in the shops for some of the books that had been mentioned and a number of the titles were no longer available.

Parents mentioned other books for children that the families had at home. These were ABC and counting books, books about animals, books about going to the dentist and to hospital, an encyclopaedia, picture dictionary and book of Bible stories. As one might expect for children of this age, other popular books contained traditional stories and nursery rhymes. The children also looked at and read reading scheme books, comics, bath books, cloth books, colour books, annuals, lift-the-flap books, books with cassettes, and books with videos.

Most books owned by the children were selected from those most readily available. This was usually from local shops, often the post office, newsagents or nearest supermarket. Some books were also bought through bookclubs, either from school or through the post, although several parents commented that these books were rather expensive. A number of parents bought books in a 'bookshop' in town (there were none locally), although most frequently this was at the Early Learning Centre, or at W. H. Smiths, chain stores that also sold other goods. Only three of the parents mentioned buying books in bookshops. Tizard and Hughes (1984) found that middle class parents tended to buy books from specialised bookshops, whereas working class parents were more likely to buy from the local toyshop or supermarket. Fewer middle class parents bought from bookshops amongst this group of families, perhaps because they all lived at a considerable distance from one. Perhaps some parents did not know about the many types of books that were available for preschool children, and therefore would not have looked out for items they did not know existed. In previous research work, I was struck by many parents' surprise at the range of books now produced for young children (Weinberger, 1988 and Hannon, Weinberger and Nutbrown, 1991).

For most of the children, the books they had at home were those that were most readily available and were relatively cheap. I suspect the books were often bought while shopping as an object, together with, or in place of, a small toy or sweets, with the child often initially attracted by a familiar character or logo on the cover. The types of picture book found in nursery and bookshops were not encountered so frequently by many of the parents and children when shopping, and also, these were often thought too expensive. Robinson and Sulzby (1984) found that the books the children liked best were mostly 'inexpensive, softbound, easily accessible books of the sort found in drugstores or supermarkets'. I think often we know intuitively that many children look almost exclusively at this type of material in their preschool years, but do not think of it in relation to what children will then experience in their early years at school, and the implications of this. I will return to this theme in Part Three of this book.

So for most children, there was a difference between what they looked at and shared at home, and what they would later find in school. In particular, the children's expectations of narrative in books arising from what they encountered at home was often different from what they would soon experience in books in the nursery. Books in nursery could be characterised as literature specifically written for children, and pitched at a developmentally appropriate level, with language that would extend and enrich their experience, neither too simple nor too complicated. These books could initially offer more meaning to readers who had had experience of similar books. Children's understanding and appreciation of texts would be enhanced both by their life experiences and by what they have absorbed from their own previous reading.

Some of the books the children had at home had either very simple captions or text, or were lengthy, wordy and possibly hard for the children, at age three, to follow. Here are some examples.

Look, look, says Jane.
Look, Peter, look.
Have a look.
Come and look.
Peter has a look.

(Murray, 1964, *We Have Fun*, p. 16)

The little pigs go
to look for a new home.

They see a man.

The man has some straw.

One little pig says,
Please give me some straw.
I want to make a new home.

(Hunia, 1977, Three Little Pigs, p. 8)

These simple texts introduce children to written narrative, but do not in themselves extend children's understanding of the potential of written language. With the Peter and Jane text, what you see is what you get. The main point of the text is in the repetition of key words, not in conveying a message. The extract from the *Three Little Pigs*, although only a little more complex than the example from *We Have Fun*, potentially provides a very different experience since those children brought up within a culture where the three little pigs is told as a story would be able to bring to it prior experience of a familiar nursery story to enliven and add detail to the few words that are given. (Of course, this is not true for all children within our society, and we should understand what a different experience this text would be for them.)

In contrast, here is a sophisticated and literary text (its adult counterpart is the adventure or horror novel). Rich in fantasy, it provides, however, quite a jump in understanding for young children who were unlikely to have acquired the wide vocabulary and extended experience of similar texts which would make it comprehensible

> In the sulphurous cavern below the mountain, Skeletor put his slaves the Skelcons to work to construct a machine which would tap the power of Eternia and convert it to energy of untold strength. Under the threat of their lord's energy-blade, the Skelcons quickly completed their task . . . a mammoth power-shield projector.
> Towering on its three telescopic legs, Skeletor's creation gleamed in the glare of the Skelcon's forge.
> 'Now we shall see who rules Eternia!' cried Skeletor, as the Skelcons swarmed over the machine to prepare for action.
>
> (Grant, 1984, Castle Grayskull under Attack! (p. 5 of 43 pages)

There is more to a text than understanding the words, and this book conveys an impression of an adventure story, enhanced by vivid pictures and possibly also lessons learned from watching programmes on a similar theme on television. Nevertheless it is a difficult text for young children, and some would find it confusing and incoherent. The extract is from a relatively long book, some forty-three pages, and if read to a three-year-old it would almost certainly be hard for them to follow and comprehend.

Both simple and difficult books of this sort are probably to be found in most homes with young children. Children often encounter a *wider* variety of books at home than in a school or nursery setting. The books children encountered at home in the Elmswood study gave them access to the world of print, to information, and to notions of being a reader. However, a gulf existed between what most of the children read at home, and the texts they would later be expected to understand at school. Some children, when hearing stories at school, would have brought with them a prior understanding of the 'rules of the game the author is playing', while others would not. Some would be able to make multiple meanings from what Margaret Meek (1988) refers to as 'polysemic texts'. By this she means texts that have several layers of meaning, making use of subtle references through style and vocabulary to other similar texts. It is the reader who actively makes the text have meaning through bringing their prior knowledge of life and the way other texts work, to make sense of the words on the page. Some children's experiences at home before school prepares them for this, but other children have yet to learn these lessons.

Comics

Children's access to printed narrative was not just through books. Even at the age of three, over a third of the children regularly looked at comics at home. While many of the children did not do this, it was only Mrs B who thought they were unsuitable:

'She's too young. She looks in the shop, but she would rip them.'

It was only for the boys that parents mentioned that they consistently bought the same comic. Those mentioned by name were *Thomas the Tank Engine*, *Thundercats*, *Dandy*, *Rainbow*, *Superman* and *A-Team*. A range of other children's comics were also bought and looked at intermittently. Much of their initial appeal probably lies in the familiarity of the characters, from popular culture and the television. Comics are a form of literacy resource found quite commonly at home, which are unlikely to be found within a nursery or school.

Telling stories

The printed word is not the only way for children to have access to narrative. Oral storytelling also fulfils this function. Parents were therefore asked if their children had stories told to them at home. Over half the parents said that this was a normal part of family life. It was usually parents who told the stories, but grandparents, siblings and other significant people who helped to look after the children did so too. The child who spoke English as a second language was told stories in her mother tongue, and a number of children also listened to stories on tapes. Stories were often told from when children were tiny. As one parent put it,

'as soon as she's realised what you've been saying, there's been people telling her stories.'

It is possible that children could make use of this oral tradition of story-telling to help them make meaning from narrative texts, particularly those that build on an oral storytelling culture such as Janet and Allan Ahlberg's *The Jolly Postman*. However, it most clearly feeds back into an oral literacy culture through children telling their own stories and re-sponding to the subsequent telling and retelling of tales.

Drawing and writing materials

There were resources for drawing and writing available to all the children. Items mentioned by the parents for children to draw and write with, or to encourage writing were:

- pencils
- crayons
- pens
- paints
- felt tips
- chalk
- drawing with a magnet
- copying shapes
- writing patterns
- stencils
- blackboard
- easel
- desk
- paper
- colouring books
- magic slates
- writing pads

Although some parents thought their children were too young to 'write', the materials were there if the child had wanted to do so. Activities such as drawing, colouring in and 'scribbling' were all regarded by the parents as normal everyday activities for the children. This list compares very favourably with the drawing and writing materials found in school. There was less variation in access to writing materials than there was for reading resources – all you need is a pen or pencil to be able to write, whereas content is embedded in reading, and type of reading material makes a considerable difference.

Games and resources linked with literacy

Family homes are often full of items that can be used explicitly for literacy learning. Many of the parents were able to give details of games and other resources linked with literacy that they used with their children at home. These included:

- games for matching, listening and sorting; for example, letter lotto game, domino game, animal sound game and shape sorters
- flash cards, alphabet cards, pictures with words underneath
- jigsaws with words, letters, or numbers
- magnetic letters
- post office set
- cutting out and sticking, including using old catalogues
- alphabet teacher (a commercial toy with moving keys that revealed words underneath letters)
- computers and toy computer
- alphabet tray, alphabet pictures, and A–Z dinner mat

This list demonstrates the variety of games and toys with literacy connections commonly found in the homes, and how well intertwined literacy is with much everyday child-rearing practice. Children learn literacy without realising it; as they play with many of their familiar games and toys, as well as deliberately having script and the nature of print pointed out to them. These are the resources the parents mentioned, although I think there were probably many other games and resources linked with literacy in the homes, but by their very familiarity, they did not necessarily spring to mind when the parents were discussing what was available to the children. Indeed, many may not have been bought to help with literacy development, although may still provide useful literacy lessons.

Television

Television was a feature in all the homes. In terms of television as a positive factor in literacy learning in this study, some parents mentioned that their child learnt to recognise words on television or Teletext, and also that they looked in the paper to find out the time of favourite programmes. A few television programmes were mentioned by parents as being helpful to literacy development, some about literacy and others more general, which parents still saw as relevant. Those specifically mentioned were *Words and Pictures* and *Adventures in Letterland*, both especially designed to teach about words and letters, *Rainbow*, an educational programme for the under fives, and wildlife programmes.

In some cases, parents mentioned television as taking the child's time and attention away from literacy activities, for example, Rob was said to be 'infatuated with TV', and did not want to move away from it, and Nigel watched a great deal of television, particularly 'soaps' at home, and limited time when he looked at books mostly to when he was at his grandparents' house. (Nigel was one of the children struggling with literacy at age seven.)

While television was sometimes a distraction, it was a factor in all the children's lives at home, and in a number of cases parents made positive comments about the role of television in relation to their children's literacy learning.

'Off the shelf' literacy packages

It is now possible to buy any number of different packages aimed at young children, to teach them to read and write in a structured and formal way. A few of the parents mentioned that they had bought some of these ready made resources to help them teach their child to read and write. Those they referred to were books for children to learn the alphabet, learn to read, learn to write (from Early Learning Centre, Ladybird books, and the local supermarket), writing patterns to copy, Speak and Spell computers, Questron books, Preschool activities, Story book, Humpty Dumpty pack (learning activities for under fives), and *Learn and Play* magazine. These types of resources were becoming increasingly prominent on newsagents' and booksellers' shelves, and the pressure on parents to buy them had increased with the introduction of the National Curriculum and scares about reading failure in the press. However, amongst the families in the Elmswood study, these sorts of resources were not widely used, and those parents who had tried them often commented that their children were still too young for them. For example, Ricky's mother said,

> 'I bought some flashcards. I've shown him the cards, but I put them away – they're too hard'

and Rachel's mother said,

> 'She's got some books to "Learn to write" and "Learn to spell". You trace over them. I started one of them, but they're too difficult. I'll save it 'til she's older.'

Mrs Y was aware that Rachel was already 'writing', and felt that what her daughter was doing herself was more appropriate at this stage of development.

> 'She has plenty of notebooks and old diaries. Her father works from home, with an office next to the playroom, and when he's working she'll get out her notebook and do her "work" – "writing" with lots of squiggles.'

There were several other examples of parents trying things, finding the children were not ready, and deciding to wait until later to do them, which demonstrates the parents' intuitive sensitivity to their child's stage of development:

> 'I'll be ready to teach him when he wants to, but you can't force it.'

The general impression created by the parents' comments was that more naturalistic activities, rather than formal ones, that fitted in more easily with other family activities, were preferred by the children. This will be discussed further when I talk about parents 'teaching' later in the chapter.

Some of the preschool children were extremely well resourced, and some children had very little, but all of them had access to reading and writing materials, and had made a start on using these resources well before their entry to nursery.

Models for literacy

When children see others at home reading and writing, they learn 'unconscious' lessons that they can then internalise about what it is to be a reader or writer. For most children, parents are their most significant role models. In the Elmswood study parents reported that all children saw them either reading or writing. However, some read and wrote considerably more than others, and some were more conscious of their role as a model for their children.

The only parent who said her son did not see her reading to herself was one of a small number of parents who had difficulties with reading. Jackie explained,

'I don't read for myself. I only read because of the children.'

Despite this, she appreciated the importance of helping her three children with literacy and was aware that they might copy her behaviour. And so she did look at books with the children, and even made the comment that

'He's got the idea of picking up a book and looking at it. He might have copied off me – seeing me pick up books.'

Four parents thought their children saw them read regularly, but did not see them write. Three other parents said they read only from newspapers or magazines. Apart from these exceptions, other parents were able to provide numerous examples of the reading and writing they were doing at home, which their children might observe.

Reading was a well-established part of most families' daily routine, and children had regular opportunities to see their parents read if not for pleasure then for practical purposes and to find out information. Some of the parents felt the pressure of time in looking after young children, and said they did not read for pleasure, often adding that they used to. Still, over half the parents said that they did read for pleasure at the time of the interview. The adults mentioned reading historical romances; for example, Jean Plaidy, Catherine Cookson, also Mills and Boon romances, and the mother from overseas enjoyed reading stories in her mother tongue. One mother liked to read non-fiction, especially biology. I asked them whether they had been read to as children themselves. Of the parents who said they did not read for pleasure, many more had not been read to as a child than those who had. There was a considerable amount of printed material regularly entering the homes. Thirty-six parents took a newspaper daily. Apart from one broadsheet paper, the others taken were tabloid or local papers. Eight families took both. In addition thirty parents took a magazine regularly. In only six families were neither daily newspapers nor magazines bought regularly, but even here, two of the families bought a paper once a week for the television listings, and two of the other families sometimes bought television guides or magazines. Also, as some of the parents commented, even without these resources, free papers and advertising brochures arrived unbidden into all the homes. Examples of items parents read, observed by their children, included:

- a whole variety of magazines read by both women and men
- books
- catalogues
- knitting and crochet patterns
- guides
- puzzle books
- professional journals and papers
- teletext
- mail

The parents also generated a long list of writing they did at home. This included:

- writing shopping lists
- bank statements
- directions
- crosswords
- keeping a diary
- appointments
- notes
- cheques
- bills
- letters
- writing for work
- word processing
- running clubs
- filling in forms and coupons
- party invitations
- writing for study
- sending for mail order items
- keeping books
- word searches
- invoice letters
- spot the ball and pools coupons
- DSS forms
- cards
- accounts
- bank paying-in slips
- desktop publishing
- writing to do with being a school governor

Some parents did only one or two of the activities listed above. Others did many, and read and wrote extensively at home.

Parents noticed that for several children, the experience of seeing a parent read or write seemed to have prompted the child to imitate their behaviour.

'I think his interest in reading come from me, probably because he sees me read a lot.'

'He gets out the Autotrader. What sets him off is my husband looking through the Autotrader.'

'She likes to watch me write a shopping list and then she "writes" hers.'

Some parents were aware of the impact of these experiences, and so they deliberately encouraged their children to participate too.

'If I'm reading a book, I'll ask him to sit and "read" with me, and he does.'

'I sell Avon now. We have a game at doing Avon. I get all the little forms out and she thinks she's helping. She loves that.'

'I type my husband's work invoices. It's ended up with buying him a typewriter because he wanted to join in.'

There was variation in the extent to which parents provided a model, along a continuum from minimal to extensive uses of literacy, but amongst this group of families, all parents at some time provided a role model in the uses of literacy for their children, and in many cases, this provided a direct observable effect on the children's literacy behaviour.

The role of brothers and sisters

Children's lives exist and develop within a particular context, which affects how they respond and interact in the world. These contexts may not be immediately obvious in a school setting, but nonetheless, they have helped to influence the experiences and outlook of the children. The role of siblings is one factor which shapes the context for a child. Nearly half the children in the study had an older brother or sister, and this had several implications for literacy in the family. Some of the parents explained that they spent time with the older child, and the child in the study joined in with them as a matter of course; for example:

'We read to her from being tiny. We always read with Robin, and she would be there too.'

'When we help Joanne to write, Sarah pretends to write too. We're telling Joanne the letters and Sarah is writing them down too.'

'He'd be in his pushchair. I'd point out signs to Rachael, and he'd look too.'

Some of the parents commented that the older siblings also provided role models which the children imitated; for instance:

'If her brother's doing homework, she'll do it too.'

'He does what she does. They sit at the table, mostly when she comes home from school.'

Because there were already children in the family, there were often books and resources for literacy available across a wider age span than in the other families. Many of the older children passed on books, or books were shared. Three of the children had access to their siblings' computers. More school-type resources were available to the children such as reading scheme books and flashcards.

Parents reported that many older siblings stimulated interest in literacy in the children in the study, and several read out loud to them. And even at three years old, four of the children in the study had started in turn to 'read' to their younger siblings.

Seven parents said that older siblings were involved in directly 'teaching' children aspects of literacy; how to read books and isolated words, how to form letters and shapes, and the sounds letters make; for example:

'If Roy's learnt a book off by heart, he learns him how to read it.'

'Kira gets hold of the flashcards and asks Nigel.'

'Lynne gives him things to do like copying letters and he does them.'

'Rachel's done a bit of sound work with him.' (Teacher's child.)

In these ways, having a sibling and being a sibling provided children with opportunities and encouragement to become involved in literacy events and practices. However, several parents explained that because they had additional children in the family, it was also true that some of the children with older brothers and sisters tended to be given less time on literacy together with their parent, compared with the time that they spent with their first child. What we need to remember is that the composition of the family has an effect on the literacy events and practices of the home, which in turn influences the children's literacy development.

Modelling adult uses of literacy in make-believe play

A number of the children engaged in make-believe play, with siblings, friends, parents, or on their own, in which the literacy practices of adults played a meaningful part. For instance, children imitated their parents' behaviour in such practices as 'reading' the newspaper, or trying out a signature:

'He'll get the newspaper, he pretends to read what's on telly, such as *Emmerdale Farm*.'

'You can see she's watched me write letters. She copies and writes loops and things across the paper and pretends to sign her name.'

Many of the children drew on a variety of adult roles in their local community as a basis for their pretend play. Among other settings they explored they played at schools, shops, libraries, cafes, and garages.

'She loves "writing". Nine times out of ten she's being a waitress, and each letter is a different mark in her notebook, "Keil will have sprouts, Terri will have ham".'

'He gets some *Autotraders* out, gets his pretend phone, and phones up, "Mark, have you seen this Range Rover? I've looked underneath, it's in sound condition".'

This type of behaviour, built upon their observations of parents and other adults in their community, or from the media, made literacy seem real to the children, and gave them another way of practising what it is to be a reader and writer.

Parents engage in literacy practices and events

Parents reading to their children

Reading to children is an end in itself rather than one of the many everyday living experiences that show children about the instrumental nature of literacy, such as shopping lists, recipes, filling in forms or reading notices. It is a very important part of children's acquisition of literacy, giving them some experience of the pleasure, information and types of language which can be derived from books.

In the Elmswood study, all but four children were read to by a parent at the time when I talked with the parents, when the children were aged three. Of these four, Gillian was sometimes read to by her aunt and grandmother, and for two of the others, Leanne and Darren, their parents had read to them in the past (when they were about two years old). This means that out of sixty children only one was not read to at home at age three. It is always hard to establish why something does not happen, but there were certain key factors which seemed to prevent these four parents from reading to their children. These included a move in haste from a difficult situation for Leanne and Darren and their mothers (and in both of these cases, although their mothers had not read to the children for a while they had done so in the past). Gillian had a medical condition which meant frequent hospital treatment that had been very disruptive during her preschool years. This seemed to have made day-to-day routines hard to establish, including the reading of stories, to which Gillian was anyway resistant. However, her mother said her aunt and grandmother read to her on occasions. These were exceptional circumstances, a medical condition and a child with pronounced interests and tolerances. The fourth child, Susan, was the youngest of four children. Her mother had over-generalised advice previously given by the teacher of her oldest daughter, which was that the school had one method of teaching reading and if something different happened at home it might confuse the child. As a result of this advice, Mrs W had subsequently 'left (the children) to pick reading up on their own'.

To summarise, disharmony in the routine of family life was a contributory factor to explain why parents of three children did not read to their children. For the remaining child, some well-intentioned but probably misleading advice was taken literally, so inhibiting literacy practices at home. This example shows just how influential information from school can be.

When someone did read to the children at home, it was mothers who did so most consistently. As I have already mentioned, all but four read to the children at the start of the study. However, it is also true that the majority of fathers also read to their children, and Kirsty's mother said that her husband read most with the child because

'he can read better than me.'

There were also other people who read to the children regularly. Parents mentioned that almost half the children were read to by a grandparent. Many of the children with older siblings were read to by them. Others who read to the children regularly were aunts, uncles, babysitters, friends, neighbours and older children visiting the family.

Parents were asked how old their child was when they were first read to at home (see Table 2). For most of the children, experience of books was an integral part of their baby and toddler years. Approximately a third of the children were under a year old when they first had the experience of being read to. About half the children were read to from the ages of one and two. For a minority, being read to at home began between the ages of

Table 2   Age from when children were read to at home

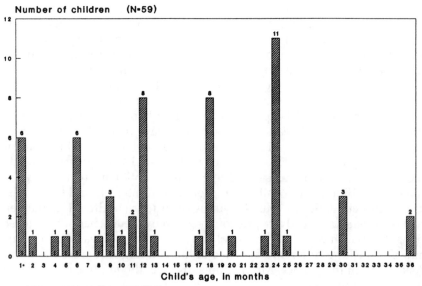

Number of children   (N=59)

Child's age, in months

* from as soon as they were born

two and three years. This gives an indication of how early the majority of parents in this study began reading to their children. For all of them (apart from one child who was not read to), being read to at home easily pre-dated their start at nursery.

When I asked parents what they read to their children, or looked at with them, it turned out that most of the children had story books and picture books read to them. Most of the children had books read to them all the way through. However, there were nine children who did not have this experience, or their parents always selected very short books with limited text, so that reading them all the way through was straightforward. Sandra's mother, for instance, said,

> 'She's got books with a picture and words underneath, and nursery rhyme books. I've got some "older" books and I'm saving them, like *Peter Rabbit* with lots of words.'

For some children, then, their access to sustained narrative, which they were to encounter at school, was severely constrained.

How often the children were read to varied. Most of the children were read to very frequently, which meant either daily, or most days, and almost a quarter were read to two or three times a week. A minority were read to less often. Two of the children were read to once a week, a further three less than that, and of course there were the four children not read to at all at the time that I talked with the parents. This begins to show the variation in experience of preschool children, and helps to explain their different responses to being read to once they start in nursery and school. Nearly half the children were read to at some time during the day, often several times a day. As far as bedtime stories were concerned, some of the children did not have a regular bedtime and other parents commented that they did not read to their children at bedtime because it made putting them to bed problematic; for instance:

> 'They don't seem to go to sleep with a story. They get too interested.'

> 'Once they have one story, they're asking for another.'

Nevertheless, having a bedtime story was part of the night-time routine for a third of the children.

Many children liked to have familiar books reread to them, and over a third of the parents mentioned, unprompted, that their child memorised the books that were read to them. The fact that so many parents spontaneously mentioned their child memorising books indicates what a visible part it played in children's literacy activities in many of the homes. Parents made comments like,

> 'When she gets used to a book, I read so much, and she'll tell you what's coming next.'

> 'With *Thomas* books, if you start a sentence, he can finish it off.'

In addition to books, a large number of children looked through mail order catalogues with their parents, and nearly half looked at magazines together. Just over a third of the children looked at comics with their parents. Seven children, all with older siblings, looked at or read reading scheme books with their parents. A number of parents mentioned looking through photograph albums together with their children. Other items mentioned were Bible stories, a children's dictionary, and adult focused material, such as newspapers, and car and motorbike brochures.

Thus children's experience of reading matter shared with them at home was varied, probably more varied than the reading materials at nursery and school, and, as well as child-centred material, included reading matter that was available and appropriate for the whole family.

Favourite books, memorising text, and acting like a reader

Many of the children, as we have seen, had what their parents would call favourite books. The children without particular favourites seemed not to have favourite books because, according to their parents' replies, books did not seem to be particularly special for them, maybe because they did not have access to many books. Eight of these children owned under a dozen books and two owned none. Only one of them was a member of the library. Parents of three of them said their child showed no or little interest in reading. Three of the mothers said they did not read to their child. It therefore seems that having favourite books could be seen to some significant extent as a consequence of familiarity with books and having the opportunity to share them within a family context.

Children can begin to see themselves as readers through memorising books, often a favourite text; for instance, one of the parents said,

> 'I think a lot of it is memory with him. We used to read nursery rhyme books to him, and when he saw the Humpty Dumpty picture, he knew what it was. Later on he knew what the simple words were.'

Without this exposure to familiar and favourite books, children did not have this opportunity.

This did not, however, prevent all but one of these children from behaving 'like a reader' on occasions. When parents were asked whether their child acted in this way, all but four parents from the whole group of sixty said their child did, and many gave examples. One child did not have favourite books, two showed little or no interest in reading and the other liked being read to, and liked to draw, but when it came to looking at books, his mother said,

> 'he likes physical things. He's not got the patience to sit down and learn.'

The ways in which parents observed their children behaving like readers varied. Most of the examples given were of children interacting with books. Over a third of the parents described the way in which children memorised books as a stage in the reading process; for example:

'He knows some books so well he will "read" you the story.'

'She knows her favourite book off by heart.'

'He always likes the same book. You'd think he could read – he knows every word.'

This exposure to books in a meaningful way, shared with family members at home, allowed for memorisation and familiarity with books and gave many of the children opportunities to experience for themselves what it felt like to be a reader.

Some of the children read to their dolls, or teddies or younger siblings; for example:

'She reads to her dolls, especially books which are really familiar to her.'

'He gets his book, and tells his teddy things.'

'Sometimes she picks up a book and pretends to read to her younger sister.'

Parents gave examples of children showing they had internalised some of the language of books, using formulaic phrases they had heard from stories; for instance:

'She makes her own words up. She always starts, "Once upon a time . . .".'

'He opens a book, and he starts "One day . . .".'

Parents had noticed how some children imitated what they had observed others do when reading, or generalised from when stories had been read to them:

'She runs her finger along the lines and pretends to read, because that's how I read it to her.'

'Especially when he's gone to bed, you find him sat with a book, talking to himself as he's looking at it.'

'She reads a lot – Little Storytellers and Thomas the Tank books. She makes up the story as she goes along.'

These children were making their own meanings as they chose, of their own accord, to interact with text.

Some parents provided examples of their children reading from printed material other than books, including newspapers, magazines, comics, trade magazines and brochures. Here parents reflected that the children had observed adult behaviour in the way they used these items; for example:

'Sometimes when he's got a comic, he's making it up. He's copying his daddy reading the paper.'

'She'll get the newspaper, look down the page and point with a finger, and say things like, "such and such is on telly at ten past ten".'

The children were not necessarily able to read the print. Rather, what was important to them was that they knew that printed texts were meaningful. For instance, although some parents gave examples of their children holding books or newspapers upside-down, the purpose of the activity, to tell a story or find out information, was always evident.

For all but four children then, behaving like a reader was a natural activity undertaken by the children at home. This provides an indication of how embedded literacy behaviours were in day-to-day life for these children, even at the ages of three.

Parents 'teaching' their children

Much of the parents' 'teaching' of literacy skills occurred in an unplanned way, usually in response to particular events or situations, and built on their child's interests. As one parent explained, 'I didn't set out to teach this or that'. There is a difference between this and much of the teaching in a school setting where objectives are usually set in advance and learning possibilities within a particular activity are specified. Learning at home has the potential to be more spontaneous, and to arise directly out of a need expressed by the individual child.

Most parents showed a sensitivity to, and awareness of, incidental activities which involved literacy learning. When I asked questions including the formal word 'teach' , this produced at times limited responses in which parents tried to fit what they did into a school learning pattern. Other more open-ended questions allowed them to give a much fuller and more realistic account of family life. These will be discussed below in the section on 'Literacy learning involved in the everyday activities'.

The 'teaching' of writing was easier for parents to identify as a deliberate act than the 'teaching' of reading. As I have already mentioned, virtually all parents read to their children. But for most, the word 'teach' implied something more structured than this. Over two-thirds of the parents said they were teaching their children to write; nearly half the parents said they were teaching their children to read; and again nearly half the parents said they deliberately pointed out environmental print to their children. In only seven families did parents say that none of these literacy skills were specifically taught.

Sometimes children resisted being taught. Three of the parents persevered trying to teach reading, and four parents continued with teaching writing, even though they felt they were battling against their child's lack of maturity and interest:

'I learn him to write his name. I hold his hand. He fights me and the pen and wants to scribble, but I do try and make him try.'

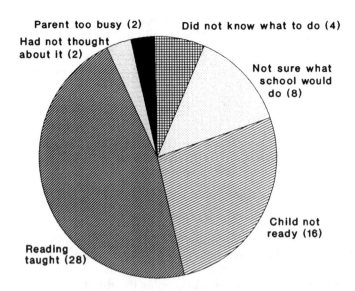

Figure 5   Parents who taught reading, and those who did not, with their reasons for not doing so

But most parents were sensitive to the developmental stage their child had reached and adjusted their input accordingly.

Nearly half the parents said that they taught their child to read, and provided examples of the ways in which they did so. (I will go into this in detail later.) However, it is also interesting to discover why some parents did not teach their child. The explanations they gave for not teaching their child to read were divided between reasons to do with the children and reasons to do with the parents (see Figure 5).

Sixteen parents thought their child was not yet ready to be taught to read. Eight of these mentioned their child's lack of interest and eight mentioned their child's lack of maturity as why they did not teach reading; the children were seen as not old enough, they did not have enough concentration, and did not have the language skills. They gave explanations like,

'He's not interested, and I'm not going to push it. If you do, they might not want to know.'

'I'll be ready to teach him when he wants to, but you can't force it.'

'I'm not teaching her at the moment – she's a bit young.'

'He likes to flit to different things.'

'He's finding it hard talking. 'Til you can talk, you can't read.'

Eight other parents felt prevented from teaching their child because of anxieties that they might not do it in a way in which the school, at a later stage, might approve; for example:

'One reason I don't teach her is I don't really understand the school's approach to learning to read. I feel I could do more harm than good.'

'I never taught the other two. I didn't know what school would do . . . It's no good him turning round to the teacher and saying, "No, you don't do it like that, my mummy says".'

One parent added the rider that teachers, not parents, get paid for teaching reading:

'I think there's plenty of time once they get to school for that. My method of teaching him to read is probably different to what you would do at school. Besides, you get paid to do that, not me.'

Four parents were uncertain about what they could do, saying, for example,

'I don't know enough about it myself.'

Two parents had not thought about teaching their child, and a further two did not do so because a heavy work schedule and domestic upheaval made it impossible at the time.

These replies give some explanation as to why it is that some parents do not feel it is appropriate for them to deliberately aim to teach their child to read, even when it turns out that most parents are doing so.

Parents appeared to be more confident about their role in teaching writing. Three-quarters of the parents said they were teaching their child to write, mostly getting their child to copy their own name. The same reasons as for not teaching reading were given for not teaching writing, although with fewer instances (see Figure 6).

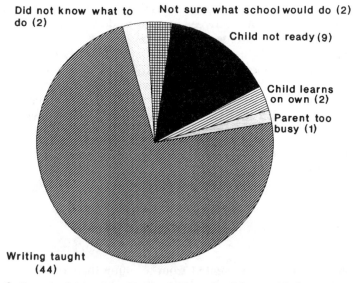

Figure 6 Parents who taught writing, and those who did not, with their reasons for not doing so

Nine parents mentioned their child's lack of interest or maturity, for example,

'She wasn't interested.'

'Not at the moment, she's a bit young. She's more interested in what's going on around her.'

'She's tried, she's not really into it yet. I'll get her something at Christmas.'

Two parents were not sure what school would do; for instance, one said,

'I don't know what to do because you don't know what they do in school. Some say "aye", "bee", "cee" (i.e. letter names), some say "ah", "buh", "cuh" (i.e. letter sounds), so I've not taught her to write her name or anything.'

Two parents were not sure what to do themselves; for example,

'I don't know what to start with.'

One parent felt too busy to teach writing. In addition two parents said they did not see the teaching of writing as necessary, but let the children get on with writing in their own way, and not intervening (although one said she did give encouragement). These, then, give some explanations as to why some parents refrain from teaching their children about writing, although, again, the majority of parents were involved in teaching their children to write.

How children were taught to read

It is interesting to know what parents of preschool children do to help their children with reading. The main strategy that the parents in the Elmswood study used was to pick out words or letters from what they were reading to the child; for example:

'I've only just started, picking little words out from what I'm reading to her.'

Ten of the parents did this. Seven parents pointed to the words as they read,

'I show him words as I read to him, I point to each word that I'm reading.'

Three parents worked with their children on the sounds that letters make, and two parents tried to see if their child could remember a story or predict what was going to happen next. Other strategies used were: playing games which involved reading, listening to story tapes together, reading things when out shopping, asking the child 'to get such and such off the shelf', using reading scheme books (*Peter and Jane, Puddle Lane, Letterland*), and asking the child to copy what the parent had read.

Only one parent, Mrs Y., responded to the question of whether she taught reading by saying yes, she had read to Robin since he was tiny, 'because that's how they learn reading (to them) isn't it?'

Most parents read to their children, but none of the others explicitly made this connection. As I have suggested before, particularly in a home context, much of the literacy teaching and learning is almost 'invisible' in that it is often not explicitly addressed, and sometimes goes unrecognised by both parents and children. This does not mean or imply, however, that few literacy practices and events take place, but rather that one sometimes has to be alert to recognise them.

What children were taught to write

In the same way as finding out more about the teaching of reading and preschool children at home, it is interesting to discover about young children's experiences of writing. Just over half the children were taught to write their name. There was often a specific purpose in this, such as children being able to label their own drawings and writing, or contribute to greetings cards:

'She likes to write her name on birthday cards.'

'He writes his name on cards, for example, to mummy from Dan.'

Other parents taught name writing for its own sake.

A few of the children taught to write their name were also taught letters or the alphabet, other family names, and how to draw particular shapes, such as circles, lines and kisses, letters of the alphabet, or short sentences about the child and family. These are all perfectly appropriate ways to initiate young children into the business and purpose of writing.

How children were taught to write

Teachers in school sometimes wish that parents would leave the teaching of writing to them, but from the numbers of parents involved with children's writing at such a young age, this seems out of tune with what is really happening in the children's homes. What is more, it is denying a tremendous resource. If teachers could communicate with parents the sorts of writing that would be useful to children in a school setting, and, more importantly, express to parents the validity in encouraging (not forcing) children's writing, allowing it to change developmentally, without the emphasis on absolute correctness as a starting point, but rather emphasising communicating meaning for a purpose, this would help foster an awareness of writing that would be useful to all children.

As to how the parents were actually teaching writing, many parents took the initiative here, and developed their own strategies for helping their child with writing. Half the children were taught to copy. A few were taught by having their hand held and guided (a couple then moved on to copying), or were taught to write over the top of the parent's writing, or over the top of lines in a book, or to follow dots to complete letters. The effect of a lack of information can lead to misconceptions on the part of parents about how writing might develop, and be taught. It would seem that more information going into homes about the stages of children's writing development and practical ways of helping children progress would be beneficial.

Parents' observations of children acting like a writer

At this stage less of the children were in their parents' views acting like 'writers' than acting like 'readers' (although in a less formal sense, all were drawing, scribbling and making marks at least on some occasions). Just over two-thirds of the children acted as a 'writer' according to their parents. Three of the four children who did not behave like readers did not behave as a writer either. However, there was no obvious pattern to characterise those children not acting as a 'writer'.

Where parents provided descriptions of their child 'writing', they noticed two distinct features. One was concerned with the reason for the activity, such as writing letters, shopping lists, names as labels and on cards, filling in forms, notes, or in pretend play; for example:

'She pretends to write a letter, put it in an envelope, and take it to Postman Pat.'

'She likes to "write" the shopping list out for Tesco (local supermarket).'

'Last time he "wrote" he said, "that's for daddy" (sometimes I leave notes for my husband when he comes back from night shift).'

'When she's done a drawing, she'll try to write her name at the top of the page.'

'I got a slip from the bank, a paying-in slip, and she wrote lots of 000s, filling the slip in.'

The other type of example was purely descriptive of what the writing looked like, with comments such as,

'She makes tiny little round shapes in long lines – she's seen me write. It's very neat, all in a straight line.'

'His writing is like little ticks and his drawing is bigger circles, and things like that.'

Parents observed that children's writing was different from their drawing (as in the example about writing and drawing above), or scribble; for instance:

'If she attempts to write, it's all dots and circles, no scribble.'

and that certain writing materials were suggestive of writing for the children; for example:

'When he's got his pencils rather than his wax crayons, he pretends to write his name.'

Unlike reading, which once done leaves no trace, writing is permanent, and parents could observe the product without being aware of the purpose. Some of the children's attempts at writing would probably have been done simply for the pleasure of creating something that looked like writing they had observed others produce, or 'double writing', as one child described it. But much of the writing was probably produced for a purpose (as most of the examples suggest), even if the parents were unaware of it.

Parents teaching children about environmental print

All the families were surrounded by environmental print, on packages, clothing, on television, in the street, in shops, on buses – none of them could avoid extensive contact. Parents were asked whether they deliberately pointed out this print to their children. Because the way children relate to such print often goes unnoticed by others or is part of taken-for-granted daily life, it was sometimes hard for parents to identify exactly what was occurring and when. Some parents felt that the way they pointed out environmental print was embedded in the way they related to their child, doing it 'unconsciously, just like mentioning colours or counting'.

Nevertheless, parents of nearly half of the children said that they deliberately pointed out environmental print to their child before they started at nursery. In their responses, parents identified a number of situations in which they were most likely to point out environmental print to their child. These were while shopping, while travelling, seeing advertisements and logos (printed and on television), and facing something potentially dangerous. Some examples are given below.

'In the supermarket I'd say, "Can you go and get me a packet of cornflakes from the shelf".'

'We're going to the butcher, you can take me. Are you sure this is the right shop?'

'If we were on the bus and I pressed the bell, I'd tell him "that says bus stopping".'

'When we were on the bus we used to look out for posters.'

'I showed her the names of shops – I was scared of her getting lost.'

'I'd point out danger signs, "what does that say?".'

'If we're ever near water, I point out instructions about the dangers.'

Response to environmental print

Many of the children were showing their parents that they responded to or could recognise environmental print at this stage:

'If she sees Tesco, it's as though she can read it.'

'If he sees signs, he'll say something related to the picture, for example, if it's of a ball, he'll say something related to a ball.'

'She often says, "that's KitKat, Oxo".'

Living in a print-rich society, children are in a position to learn early lessons from the print in their environment. Parent comments here show how they had taken note of their children's awareness of this print, although much that the children absorbed would be more likely to go unrecognised, if not vocalised, during these early stages.

The teaching of nursery rhymes

As I have discussed in Chapter 4, familiarity with rhyme has been shown to be very helpful for children's early reading development. For this reason, I asked parents about the nursery rhymes and rhyming they shared with their children. All the parents said they recited at least one nursery rhyme with the children when they were very little. Some children knew a considerable number of rhymes, some up to a dozen, while two children knew only one or two. A few parents mentioned playing with rhyme with their child; for example:

'When I read a nursery rhyme, I follow along with my finger and miss the last word off, to see if she can finish it.'

'We'd play silly nursery rhymes. I'd deliberately miss things out and he'd chuckle about that.'

Some parents were able to give specific examples of the way their child responded to rhyme; for example:

'He memorises a story and can turn the pages and "read" it, especially if it rhymes.'

The majority of parents said that their children were able to distinguish words that rhymed, and were able to recognise, say or invent rhyming words; for example:

'I used to sing nursery rhymes all the way through, and if I said something wrong she'd pick me up and say, "no, it's not like that".'

'He was brilliant with his nursery rhymes, he knew them off by heart.'

'He could make up silly words of his own and they would always rhyme.'

Parents of only seven children said they thought their child was not able to do this. For nearly all the children, then, parents observed and often encouraged a familiarity with rhyme within a home context. This was probably never done with the intention of helping with their children's literacy, although it is more than likely that this was its effect.

The parents of only seven children said their children were not sensitive to rhyme, and not able to discriminate between words that rhymed and those that did not. Of these, one only knew

'the first two lines of baa baa black sheep'.

Five knew up to a dozen, and one knew a large number of rhymes. So experience of nursery rhymes was one that all the children shared, but to varying degrees, from extremely limited, to extensive and familiar contact.

Parents' observations of children's initiative in literacy practices

Many parents gave instances of children taking the initiative in literacy practices and events. They were not passive recipients of literacy experiences at home, but were active learners. Most children were engaged and interested, at least in some aspects of literacy, and this tended to be what the majority of parents expected, rather than what they were surprised by. As one parent put it, when asked about her child's interest in literacy,

'I thought it was natural.'

Parents also pointed out that children of this age would not do anything that they did not want to do. Some of the children took the initiative and asked their parents to be involved in an aspect of literacy with them; for example:

'He insists on his bedtime story.'

'She comes to us and asks us what the words are.'

'We do writing together when she asks.'

'She often says, "what does that say?" like a sign on a bus or in a shop, and I tell her.'

Parents of two-thirds of the children noticed that they were involved in literacy activities, whether 'reading' or 'writing', on their own, and at their own initiative, either daily or most days. A small group of eight children 'read' or 'wrote' on their own either only once a week or less. This was therefore not a regular activity for them, and points to the diversity of experience within the homes.

Literacy learning in everyday activities

One of the strengths of the home is that it offers children an opportunity for uncontrived learning situations. Much occurs naturally, without parents consciously noticing that it is helpful for literacy, since the transmission of literacy often 'occurs at the margins of awareness' (Leichter, 1974). Nevertheless, unprompted, the list of what the parents themselves picked out as being helpful to their children's literacy development was substantial, wide ranging and often embedded in everyday family activities. When asked about resources and activities helpful for children's literacy development, parents demonstrated a broad interpretation of what was useful for literacy in their replies. The illustrations given in Table 3 combine to give a flavour of the sorts of things that were happening at home. Achieving literacy is not only about interacting with books and writing materials, but also about skills acquired in the ordinary activities of everyday life. These events and practices are not separate and special, but indistinguishable from the rest of their lives. They have meaning and purpose because they are an integrated part of daily life. Table 3 shows examples of everyday activities reported by parents as encouraging children's literacy development.

Table 3   Everyday activities that encourage children's literacy development

- Writing and drawing in steam on the windows
- Selecting shopping by the label
- Writing a shopping list
- Writing names in cards
- Child writing their name on drawings
- Reading and writing alongside their parent
- Reading letters to the child
- Cutting and sticking using old catalogues
- Watching television together
- Reading things off the television
- Following up ideas from children's television programmes
- Recognising product labels
- Baking
- Modelling with plasticine and playdough
- Taking the child out
- Saying and singing nursery rhymes
- Listening to cassettes with songs
- Operating washing machine: 'Gareth can operate the washing machine by himself. If it say "do an F wash", he can switch it on and do all the instructions in the right order.'
- Using a home computer
- Filling in bank paying-in slips
- Putting laundry away
- Looking at pictures
- Looking at photo albums

The difference between families was again evident, with some parents involving their children in many activities, and others doing only a little. But it is worth pointing out that something was going on in each of the homes.

As schools become more standardised and oriented towards specific goals, the distinction between the informal literacy learning at home and the more formal literacy learning and teaching at school might widen. The pressure to standardise what is available at home has begun to filter through from the National Curriculum, the media, and the proliferation of products designed to help parents 'teach' their children. It would be a loss if what is already happening was not acknowledged and built upon by schools and teachers.

Summary

What were the literacy environments of children at home, before nursery?

Children's involvement in literacy practices and events came in the main from three sources. The first was literacy resources being available: books, other printed material, and resources for writing in the home. The second involved being part of the literacy environment at home, following the examples of parents, siblings and others. Finally, there was engagement in activities which gave rise to some form of literacy behaviour, such as shopping, bus rides, outings and games.

These opportunities varied, as did the children's own inclinations. Many children were involved in a number of different literacy activities at home, and minimal involvement was unusual within the group. While the group represented a span of interest and opportunity, the main message of the study at this point is that on the whole, the children had learned a considerable amount about literacy at home by the age of three.

Resources and opportunities for literacy

While there was wide variety of experience between families, with many providing rich and complex environments for literacy, and a few offering less, all the children had literacy experiences at home.

Reading and writing materials were available in all children's homes, although the range varied considerably between families. All children had access to some children's books. Nearly a third owned more than 50 books, but a couple owned none at all. Only about a quarter of the children were library members, and these included the children who already owned the most books. Two-thirds of the children were said to have favourite books. Only eight of these favourites were books of the type found in nursery, so there was a difference between what the children read at home and what they would later encounter at nursery and school. Children had access to a wide range of other printed material. Resources for drawing and writing were available for all children, and parents regarded drawing, colouring in and 'scribbling' as standard activities.

Literacy models

All parents reported that their child saw them reading or writing at some time, although some did a great deal more than others, and some were more conscious of their role as a literacy model. Only four parents said they did not read anything other than newspapers and magazines at home. Children used observations of parents and others in their make-believe play. Older siblings often acted as literacy models.

Parents' interactions with literacy activities with their children

Parents read at home with most of the children, and other children were read to by family or friends. Parents of just over a third of the children read to them from before their first birthday, while parents of a small minority of children only started reading to them between the ages of two and three. Most children had books read to them all the way through, but a minority only had sections of books read to them, or were read to from specially chosen short texts.

Nearly half the parents said they deliberately pointed out environmental print to their child before nursery. All parents said they recited at least one nursery rhyme with their child when they were very little. Much parental teaching of literacy skills occurred in response to particular events or situations, was directly relevant to the child, and was embedded within ordinary day-to-day activities.

What had children learned about literacy at home, before and after nursery?

All children in the Elmswood study had learned something about literacy and had developed literacy skills before joining nursery, and therefore well before their start of compulsory schooling.

The majority of the children had favourite books, or access to a number of books they liked. The small proportion of children without favourites were those who tended to own fewer books, were unlikely to be library members, and had less opportunity to share books within a family context.

Virtually all children behaved 'like a reader' on some occasions, and just over two-thirds behaved like 'writers'. They 'wrote' for a purpose, attempting such things as letters or shopping lists.

Parents of nearly half the children gave examples of them responding to environmental print. Just over a quarter of the children knew a large number of rhymes, while two children knew only one or two. The majority of children were able to distinguish words that rhymed, through recognition, repeating or inventing rhyming words, while a small number of parents thought their child was not able to do this.

In this chapter we have begun to see quite how rich the home environment is for most children at the early stage of their literacy learning. In the next chapter we meet the same children again, four years later.

6

Literacy at Home: Children Aged Seven

What changes in the course of four years growing up, and what remains similar? In the last chapter, through the parents' eyes, we saw what the children's homes were like as contexts for literacy learning for three-year-olds. In this chapter we look again at broadly the same issues, using the parents' observations to highlight in what ways homes provided a literacy learning context once these same children had reached the age of seven. By this stage of the Elmswood study there were forty-two children who had been part of the study for four years (see Appendix 2). There were now twenty-four boys and eighteen girls. Thirty-five children went to the school where they had been to nursery, and seven children had moved to other schools, each one to a different school.

Parents provide resources and opportunities for literacy

As in the previous chapter, we look first at children's books in a home context.

Buying and owning books

By the time the children were aged seven, all but one of the parents bought books for them. Only two of the children, according to their parents, appeared indifferent to this. One child, James, already had a large number of books, but was not showing much interest in them. He had had 'hundreds' of books bought when he was little, but 'was not terribly grateful'. Mrs E., his mother, said that he 'wouldn't appreciate a book for a present'. There was another child, Mark, who had books bought for him, but was not keen on them. As his mother said, 'he'd rather get a car'.

Ten of the parents bought their children books only from local shops, for example, at the newsagents, post office and supermarket, where the choice was limited. Many of their children were among the group of poorest readers. But the pattern of book buying had changed since the children were three. This was partly because schools had had an impact on book buying for children through school bookclubs. They had selections of books similar to those found in bookshops and in schools available for sale, together with savings stamps for the books. In addition at least five of the eight schools that the children went to held annual bookfairs where large numbers of children's books were displayed, which could be purchased. Nearly half of the parents said they sometimes bought books from their child's school club, and parents and children also mentioned buying books at school bookfairs. School bookclubs and annual bookfairs greatly increased the range of children's books available locally, although a couple of parents commented on the cost of these books, 'I think they're a bit steep', and 'I thought they were quite expensive'. Three of the parents bought children's books from bookclubs other than those run by school. Other parents bought books in town, usually at shops that also sold other goods, such as W. H. Smith or the Early Learning Centre. In addition to the ten parents who only bought their children's books locally, another five parents also mentioned buying children's books in local shops. Other places to buy books mentioned by parents were the main market, car boot sales, jumble sales, and bring and buy stalls. Seven of the forty-two parents said they bought most children's books in bookshops. A few of the children were very familiar with bookshops. As one of the parents said,

'We could leave them (the child and her sister) all day, and they wouldn't know we'd gone',

but for the majority of the children in the Elmswood study, going to a bookshop was something that was infrequently or never done.

By the age of seven, all the children owned some books of their own. Only three children had no more than a dozen books (they were all poor readers), while over half the children owned more than fifty books each. This information appears in Table 4.

Borrowing books

There had been just a slight increase in library membership amongst the group by the time children were aged seven. Eight children who had not been members at three had now joined the library, although there were also three children who were no longer members. Their reasons for not being a library member any more varied. One of the parents gave no particular explanation, one thought that the school provided as good an access to books as a library could, and the third had not transferred to another library since the nearest one had closed as a result of cuts in local services – a story which I am sure has been repeated in many other places. Some parents took their children to the library very frequently. A couple of children borrowed library books more than once a week, and four children were taken to the library every two or three weeks. Other

Table 4   Book ownership and library membership of children aged seven

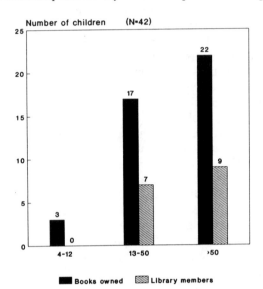

children went to the library less often. Two of the children were taken to the library less frequently than they had done before since the closure of the nearest library. One parent explained the difference:

'Now you have to go out of your way to go.'

As at the age of three, children who owned the most books were also more likely to be library members, and so had good access to children's books, while there was still a small minority of children who had extremely restricted access to books at home (see Table 4).

Favourite books

Most parents said that their children had favourite books, and for many of those without particular favourites, they had plenty of books to choose from. The types of books mentioned as favourites gives an indication of the sorts of reading material characteristically available to the children. The range was wide, from nursery rhymes and books with simplified texts right through to children's novels. In some cases the children read the book themselves to themselves, and in some cases it was read to them.

The range of different sorts of books children had as favourites had been extended since the children started at school. Nearly half the children now had the sorts of picture books, well-crafted and thoughtfully presented, commonly found in nursery and infant schools as favourites. Some of these had been bought at the school's bookclub, and for one of the children, Katherine, her two favourites were picture books familiar to her from school. Some children had fairy tales or nursery rhyme books as favourites.

Three children had longer children's novels as favourites. Roald Dahl was Nicky's favourite author, *The Twits* specifically and his novels generally, Samantha had several favourites, including Dick King-Smith's *Sophie's Tom* and *Sophie's Snail*, and *Gobbolino the Witch's Cat*, and Rachael had Jill Murphy's *The Worst Witch* as a favourite. Although all these books were available in the focus school in the study, children could only choose to have them as a 'reading book' once they had completed their progress through the twelve stages of the reading schemes, so in actual fact access to these books was restricted.

One child, Sarah, had included among her favourites the book she had also liked the best at three, *The Tiger who Came to Tea*. Other parents also mentioned that the children liked to return to books they knew well, saying, for example,

'He still goes back to the old ones.'

'She still goes back to the Happy Family books.'

A third of the parents mentioned picture books that one would be unlikely to find in school as their children's favourite. These often had characters in them from television programmes or films, for example *Turtles* (Dave and Leroy's favourite books), *Thomas the Tank* and *Postman Pat* (favourites for Mathew and Rick), *Flintstones* (Ellie's favourite) and *Dumbo* (Leanne's favourite). Non-fiction books were mentioned as favourites for four children. These were a *Beano* annual (Dick), a ghost joke book (James), a child's dictionary (Richard), and a book about wrestling (John). As you can see, all these children were boys. Other studies have shown boys' preference for non-fiction reading material (for instance, White, 1990, Millard, 1994). Again most of these books differed from the ones commonly found in school. The preference for books that were only available in a home setting illustrates one of the differences that can be found between the literacies of home and school.

One parent, Mrs T, said her daughter (Joanne) had a reading scheme book, *Roger Red-hat*, as her favourite book. This was indicative of the lack of choice Joanne had in reading material, since there were few children's books for her at home. Since she was not familiar with many different kinds of books, her range of choice was particularly restricted. The pictures form a large part of the 'text' of this book, but nevertheless, the words show how limited the material was for a book to have as one to return to and learn about the nature of responding to texts, as one does with a favourite book. Here are the first five pages:

Roger Red-hat

Here is Roger Red-hat

Roger's hat

Here is Roger's hat.
Roger's hat is red.

Rip

Rip is Roger's dog.

Mr Red-hat

Here is Mr Red-hat

Mrs Red-hat

Here is Mrs Red-hat.

(McCullagh, 1969, pp. 1–5)

If Joanne's favourite book was a stylised reading scheme book, probably chosen because it was the only book she felt she could 'read' herself, what impression was she likely to have had of what reading is for, and what it has to offer her? Needless to say, Joanne was a child who struggled with her reading.

There were two girls with a wide experience of different sorts of books at home, who voiced criticisms of the reading scheme books they were presented with at school, when compared with their favourite books at home. Rachael thought the books in school were boring, and she said she got 'fed up' with reading them. Asked what she preferred, she said she liked to read

> 'normal books, like *Red Riding Hood* and *The Three Bears*. I get them at home. There are no books I like to read here (i.e. at school).'

Samantha did not like reading from scheme books because she did not like the characters, and often felt the stories were inconsistent:

> 'some have got stories at the end that aren't like what they say on the front.'

Her own choice of favourite, King-Smith's *Sophie's Snail*, did not, she felt, have these shortcomings. Here is a child who has learned to read the messages of a book's covers, setting up expectations in her that were not met by the reading scheme material she had access to.

These two children were among the better readers. Their comments indicate that they were not being satisfied or stretched at school in terms of reading. Ms N., Nicky's mother, said Nicky also preferred the books she read at home to the ones from school,

> 'She likes to pick out her own. I have to buy certain ones to appeal to her . . . like Enid Blyton novels or books by Roald Dahl . . . She wouldn't choose the ones from school, probably the way they're presented.'

When I talked with the children, this dissatisfaction was not widely voiced. This begs the question of whether other children did not express dissatisfaction with reading scheme books because they were happy with them, because they took them for granted, because they offered support to the less confident readers, or because the children's lack of experience with many other sorts of books led them to accept what they knew best. This, of course, is entirely speculation. Also, there is a great range of reading scheme books, often with newer titles having more engaging story lines than some of the older scheme books. However, I do think that while reading schemes are a useful resource to supplement other reading materials, as virtually the sole type of book given to children on which to learn how to read and practise reading, they have many inadequacies when compared with reading material children want to, and need to, read for 'real' reasons other than practising the skill of reading. As Dombey (1992, p. 22) suggests,

> No scheme book can teach a child that the words on the page can be savoured, or can yield richer meanings on a second reading.

This lack of sufficiently stimulating material for children to read in some scheme books points to the need to supplement them from other sources.

What other sorts of print do children read?

Once the children could read silently, much of their reading could occur unnoticed. Parents were asked for examples of what the children read for themselves, and because of the sometimes invisible nature of this activity, there was likely to be under-reporting here. All the children had access to a wide range of different sorts of printed material at home. The examples of this print that the parents gave provide a flavour of the sorts of material children were reading. They mentioned:

- comics
- newspapers (as one parent said, 'he'll read newspapers 'til there's no print left')
- puzzle books and crosswords
- trade magazines
- mail order catalogues
- TV listings, Ceefax and Oracle
- football magazines, football cards
- maps
- cereal packets
- seed packets (Adam, whose grandfather involved him in gardening, could 'read the back of a packet of seeds and know what to do').

What we see here is probably a different, and possibly wider, range of printed material than most children commonly make use of in school. This is the sort of print which is commonly found in many homes, which is part of the texture of everyday life, often without thought of the literacy implications. At home, children interact with this world of print which is often initially geared for adult consumption. At school, the print children encounter may well be more closely targeted for a particular age range. Both types of print have their place, but it is worth bringing their inherent difference consciously to attention so that we see more clearly the different print worlds which children inhabit.

Parents observing children's reading: what do the parents see?

A few parents thought their child was behaving like a reader, without actually reading, for example,

'I don't think he's reading, he's just looking at the pictures'

while other children clearly demonstrated that they knew how to read for themselves. For example, one parent said her daughter had explained that, 'I'm reading in my mind.'

When children spent time with books, what was it that they were reading? All but four of the parents observed that their children read to themselves, most commonly from their own books, which were usually story books. These varied in type from very short simple texts, such as Murray (1964) Peter and Jane *We Have Fun*, or *The Three Little Pigs* (both Ladybird), to complex and extended texts, for example Roald Dahl (1980) *The Twits*, or Janet and Allan Ahlberg (1986) *The Jolly Postman*. The language complexity, story structures and style of presentation varies considerably. The intertextuality of *The Jolly Postman* relies upon children's prior knowledge of nursery rhymes and fairy stories, so that they can understand the references and play on words in the story. The Ladybird version of *The Three Little Pigs* is also dependent upon the child's familiarity with the story to flesh out its meanings. However, a text like *We Have Fun* provides no intertextuality.

Again many of the books the parents mentioned that their children read were those that were most readily available, particularly those books published by Ladybird Books. Several children also had books accompanied by tapes on which to listen to the story. Several parents, mainly of boys, mentioned a number of non-fiction books. These were: dictionaries, joke books, books of films ('If he's seen the film he'll look at the book'), books about cars, computer books, a book about wrestling, one about gymnastics, and one about football.

At this stage, all but one of the parents thought their child could and did read print in the environment. Nigel was one of the children who was having difficulties with reading at seven, and his mother commented, 'I'm not sure that he can recognise it.' Although the other parents thought they knew their child could read environmental print, they mostly did it in their heads by this age, so it was hard for parents to give examples of them doing it. One of the children, however, explicitly told me, 'When we go shopping, I read all the things I see' and another said he read 'things that say on my shirts', meaning that he read the writing on his sweatshirts.

All but one of the children helped themselves freely to books when they chose to. In this case, Kyle had two younger siblings and his mother was concerned that they might rip the books. She therefore stored all the books on a shelf out of reach and Kyle asked when he wanted a book for it to be handed to him. In this way he was dependent on an adult for access to books. Some of the other families kept some of the children's books at home out of range too, but on the whole children had ready access to books if they wanted to read or look at them.

Where the books were kept at home varied, and included the main living area, the child's bedroom or playroom, and 'all over the house'. Books were most commonly kept on bookshelves. In a few families, however, books were stored indiscriminately with toys or other objects such as in a toy box, or together with toys behind the settee and under the stairs, in drawers or in a wardrobe. (These families also tended to store their resources for drawing and writing in a similar way.) For these few children, their books were not treated as different from other objects in their possession, and had the same status as other playthings. Five of these children were among the children with literacy difficulties. This may well have affected their view of the *function* of books, in that they may have been more likely to treat them primarily as objects rather than as sources of entertainment or information.

Drawing and writing materials

Resources which encouraged drawing and writing were available to all the children, just as when they were aged three. They helped themselves from a range of resources which included:

- pens, pencils, coloured pencils, crayons
- felt tips, biros, marker pens, highlighter pens
- ink, chalks, paints, oil paints
- rulers, set of compasses, set squares, rubbers, stencils
- sellotape, string, staples, paperclips
- plain paper, lined paper, squared paper, notepads
- books, files, little books, exercise books, scrap paper
- folders and a ledger from their parents' work
- colouring books, dot-to-dot books
- puzzles, quizzes, word searches
- a spirograph, typewriters
- desks and a briefcase.

Some children had a wide range of resources to choose from, while others had more limited choice, but the opportunity to draw and write whenever the child wanted to was available to all. Some parents commented on how easy access to drawing and writing resources was for the children, saying, for example, 'they're always at hand' and 'he doesn't have to look far'.

Some children at the age of three were already making distinctions between different writing resources, but this discrimination was, as you might expect, even more marked at seven. Some parents, for instance, specifically said their child now preferred to write in pen rather than pencil, which they had used more at an earlier stage. This showed increasing awareness on the children's part of the craft of writing as undertaken by more experienced writers. For example, parents commented,

'She thinks she's more grown up if she's using ink.'

'She's got a thing for "real writing" and joining letters up. It used to be crayons and felts. Now it's very much pens.'

'Probably because his dad would use a pen, he'd use one.'

This increased discernment, needing 'the right tool for the job', was also reflected in other selections of writing resources that children made; for instance, one parent described her son's make-believe play,

'If he's doing things for his club, he needs the paper to be the right size.'

One child preferred to write with pencil rather than pen, but again, the tool was chosen for a specific reason:

'He usually likes to write with a pencil – he can rub it out if he gets it wrong.'

These observations made by the parents show that they were aware of providing writing resources for the children, with a slightly different range of materials than those commonly found in school, and that they were also aware of their children's use of the resources.

Parents observing children writing

Parents noticed that all but two of their children wrote on their own at home by the age of seven. One of these two children, however, did write his name on cards for special occasions such as birthdays and wedding anniversaries. Both these two children were among the weakest in both reading and writing at age seven. A further child, Rick, who was also poor at reading and writing, liked to copy write and 'pretend' to write (his parents' description), but could not yet write in a conventional way independently. He would copy from his sister, or the newspaper, and show his mother, 'Look what I've done mum', and then ask, 'What does it say?'

Copying is a very different writing skill from composing one's own text. When copying the children practise motor skills and hand-eye co-ordination. In composing, however, the child is engaged in a level of abstraction where he or she 'must disengage himself from the sensory aspect of speech and replace words by images of words' (Vygotsky, 1962, p. 98). So we can see that within this frame of reference, Rick found the abstract nature of composing too difficult, although he did understand that written language had meaning.

A popular activity was story-writing, with over half the children com-posing stories at home expressing their own ideas independently. Their

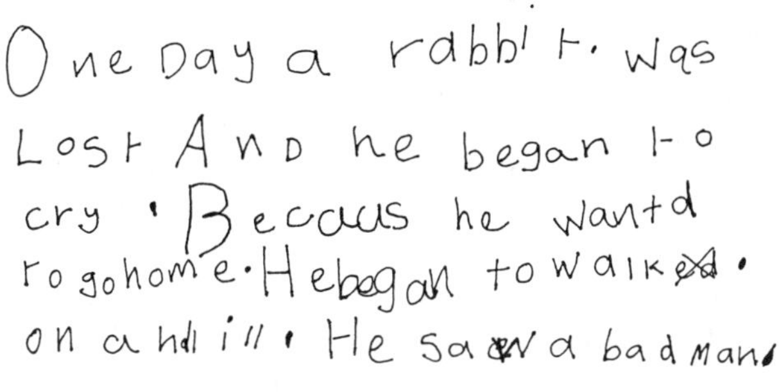

One Day a rabbit. Was
Lost And he began to
cry 'Becaus he wantd
ro gohome. He began to walked.
on a hill. He saw a bad Man

Figure 7 Example of a child's story written at home, at age seven

influence here could have been writing done at school, or could have been a desire to express ideas as a result of contact with the storying process at home and at school. Many parents made comments like

'She likes to write stories that she makes up herself.'

'He makes little stories up.'

Katy, for instance, recalled in full a story that she had made up at home:

'I wrote about a butterfly. It was about a caterpillar, and it went for a walk and he met a butterfly and he said, "I wish I was nice and purple like you", and then he met a blue bird and he said, "I wish I was blue and I could fly like you", but one day he built a cocoon round him and he turned into a caterpillar, and he were a butterfly . . . And I drew a picture at the bottom, and my mummy saved it and put it in the journal.'

(The journal was Katy's mother's record of all her children's achievements.)

This story clearly shows the influence of other stories Katy had heard and read; for instance, Maris (1988) *I Wish I Could Fly*, and Carle (1974) *The Very Hungry Caterpillar*. Here she had internalised story patterns and was able to reproduce them in her own work. She also knew, because of the journal, that her mother valued her accomplishment.

Figure 7 shows an example of another child's story, which Rachael's mother saved and clearly valued.

Many children liked copying someone else's writing, copying the craft of writing and practising being a writer rather than primarily using writing for a purpose. Most frequently this was copying out of their own books, including from a dictionary. Sometimes the children asked their parents to write something which they then copied. Some of the children copied writing from the newspaper, and the writing out of old birthday cards. An exception was Laura. Her mother had noticed that she was using copy writing for a very specific purpose. She was waiting for her mother to have a new baby, and was preparing a welcoming gift:

'I'm making a book for it, *Winnie the Pooh's Blowy Day.* I'm copying words and pictures.'

This activity showed that for Laura, a homemade book of one's own was clearly something very valuable and special within a family context.

Over half the children who wrote at home wrote specifically to communicate with someone else, usually to family or friends, in the form of letters, notes and cards. For instance, parents recalled,

'She writes little letters to her uncle. She wrote a letter to grandma about mum and dad. We were arguing. She wrote it all down.'

'She writes little love notes – I love you – and posts them under the door in a morning.'

'He made his own mother's day card.'

One parent showed me an example of one of the many 'I love you' notes she regularly received (see Figure 8).

Figure 8   Example of a child's note written at home, at age seven

Several children mentioned writing letters at home; for instance:

'I write letters to my friends in the holiday'

and one of the children, Sam, wrote to someone outside his immediate circle, while on a family holiday to Disneyland:

'. . . about Mickey Mouse and (I) took it to his dressing room. He said, "that's very good, Sam." I wrote, "To Mickey Mouse, I liked your clothes, Sam".'

Here, writing had a role to play within the context of a family holiday.

Several of the parents noticed that their children wrote factual accounts, often accompanied by a drawing. They wrote about things they had done, or descriptions of themselves in their world. Quite likely this was modelled on writing done at school. For example, parents said

'If she's been with her nanan for the weekend, she'll write what she's done and do a picture.'

'If they go on a school trip, he writes about his school trip.'

'At the weekend she wrote on the computer, "My name is Laura. I have a rabbit. Luke had a rabbit. I am 7. My rabbit eats kabj and carits".'

One of the parents commented that her child also added items she had collected such as postcards and feathers to writing she did on holiday. There were a number of children who wrote lists to create a concrete record of what they wanted, or had on their mind; for example, parents said

'He wrote his own Christmas list. It took about half an hour. He really wanted to do that – the longest time I'd seen him writing.'

'If she had something in mind, she'll write a list of what she wants, like her list for Easter was Matchmakers, Yorkie, mini eggs, All Gold and a Bart Simpson Egg.'

'He writes his own shopping lists.'

This purposeful writing was also highlighted by James's parent who described how James would not write for the sake of it, but would write if it was integrated into what he was otherwise doing:

'He wouldn't sit and write a story or write on his drawings if he drew a house, but if he's playing a game where you have to leave messages, or playing at clubs with kids in the road and they write down who's in it, he'll do that writing – writing for a purpose.'

These examples clearly show how the purposeful nature of young children's writing was integrated into their day-to-day lives and their play in a home and community context.

A few parents noticed that their children added written labels or talk bubbles to their drawings. Three children liked to write their name, names of people in their family, or their name and address. Leanne's mother had saved her drawings of small pictures of herself and her family, with the initial letter of each person above or underneath. Parents also gave other examples of writing. These included two children who made their own games, one involving writing on big pieces of paper, the other, devising a game using letters. Two other children liked to fill in forms, one child wrote her own contributions to a 'journal' in which her mother recorded other family events, and one child wrote a diary. Parents of two of the children observed that they showed the level of independence in writing that they had reached. While most children asked adults or siblings for help if they did not know how to spell a word, or had a go on their own, these two would look in their picture dictionary, or other books of their own, to see if they could find the correct spelling.

Four parents (three of weak readers) commented that their child 'pretended' to write rather than writing as such. For two of these children the comment was made in the context of make-believe play, pretending to write letters and prescriptions at an office or at the doctor's. The other two children had writing problems. While other parents accepted their children's contributions as writing, even if they could not decipher them, these children were not seen as writers by their parents, and their efforts were not afforded the status of 'real' writing. Although this is speculation, it may even be that the children's literacy difficulties were not helped by their parents' lack of recognition of the literacy practices the children actually engaged in.

Games and resources linked with literacy

As well as supplying the children with books and writing materials, most parents deliberately provided other resources to help their children with reading and writing. Those that they specifically mentioned were:

- commercially produced books in which children finish or copy words
- toy computers with reading games
- flashcards, commercial and homemade
- story and rhyme tapes
- typewriters
- magnetic letters
- games connected with reading including:
- Scrabble
- The Game of Knowledge and similar games where the child had to read the questions
- Spellmaster
- picture word cards, picture snap
- pairs, dominoes with words
- Questron books with games and spellings

Several parents also mentioned playing non-commercial games with a literacy content, such as sending messages to one another, playing I-Spy and hangman.

In connection with the commercially produced materials, a number of the parents voiced dissatisfaction, because they failed to hold the children's interest, commenting, for example,

> 'I bought three packs of writing books from the Early Learning Centre. We got to the first page and didn't go beyond that. It was a waste of money.'

> 'We got about half a dozen books from the Ladybird reading system. I didn't carry on for very long. I felt she was developing without it and it was counterproductive to what she was doing at school. The flashcards were useful to build up her vocabulary, especially common words, but the stories weren't interesting enough.'

Although these products had seemed attractive, they did not seem to hold the children's attention in the way that materials with a less obviously didactic focus were able to do.

At the time of the Elmswood study, the use of computers was just beginning to become more widespread within families' own homes, and indeed many parents felt their children were able to learn about some aspects of literacy from their use of computers. Two-thirds of the children had access to a computer at home. Of these, parents said only six used the computer solely for games without a keyboard, and consequently their parents did not think they learned anything about reading and writing from them. For the rest, items parents mentioned that the children were learning were keyboard skills, recognising words on the screen, spelling, learning simple words, typing instructions for loading software, and using a variety of programmes, for instance, making a newspaper, designing cards, playing a shopping game, finding letters to a time limit, and playing educational games such as Granny's Garden and Pod. Some of the children used the computer for writing names and other words they knew, and for writing their own stories. A couple of parents mentioned that the computer helped to give their child confidence in writing, saying, for example,

'She sits and writes a story on the computer. It's helped her a lot. She gets upset because she can't write neatly and her letters are back to front.'

It is interesting here how conscious parents were of the literacy aspect of computer use and how both at home and at school the use of IT is increasing rapidly. Often the type of computer and its uses vary from home to school settings, showing again different aspects of literacy reflected in different contexts.

Literacy models

Family members as models for literacy

Parents and others at home can influence a child's views of literacy, and their literacy behaviour, through their literacy practices, whether or not what they do is consciously directed at supporting children's literacy. The children were asked how aware they were of others reading and writing at home. Only seven children could not provide examples (and four of these were amongst the children with literacy problems). Most of the children commented on observing reading and writing for a specific purpose, including for work (and homework); for instance,

'My mum reads cookery books. She writes out of the book what she's going to do and then she puts the book away (when she's finished, she puts it in the bin).'

'Mum and Dad read letters and Mum writes to her friends.'

'My Dad normally reads the newspaper.'

'Sometimes my Dad reads special books, like from the bank.'

'Mum writes lists for Tesco.'

'Mum and Dad write notes for each other if they're going out.'

'Mum writes things when something's gone wrong, like we got butter with sellotape in, and she wrote to complain.'

Other members of the family were also mentioned as models, for example:

'My sister has to write a lot of words for homework. She's in the "comp".'

'My sister's on her exams now and she reads loads of books.'

'Grandad writes down telephone numbers.'

Other examples that the children gave were about reading and writing for recreation, such as

'My dad reads big books. Some are horror ones and some are comedy ones. One has something like a hobgoblin on the cover. He's got a lot more ones than horror ones.'

'My Mum does her crossword sometimes.'

'My brother reads adventure books from the library at school.'

There were clear gender differences in some of the replies that children gave, which indicates that from a young age children often see men and women use reading and writing in different ways. The children commented that their mothers read newspapers, books generally, and 'women's books', cookery books, baby books, college books, and letters from friends. In terms of writing, the children said they saw their mothers doing the crossword in the paper, they wrote shopping lists, recipes, kept track of knitting, they wrote notes to members of the family and to school, letters to friends, college assignments, letters of complaint and kept a journal.

The fathers also read newspapers, including one child who said his father read 'rude papers with ladies with no clothes on', and many read books, including computer books, war and army books, horror books, comic books and one child mentioned 'one about the Titanic, how it sunk and everything'. Several children mentioned that their fathers wrote for work; for instance, 'he writes about his work and how many things he's done, and how much they've got to pay him'. They also wrote letters, and noted down videos.

One child summarised the differences between the content of men's and women's reading, as noticed by many of the children, in his observation that

'I see them reading in bed. My mum reads books with roses on (presumably he is referring to Mills and Boon romantic novels), and my dad reads monster books and computer books.'

These examples demonstrate how observant the children were. In these many ways, other members of the family acted as literacy models for the children, and many of their literacy practices were indeed reflected in the children's own behaviour in terms of literacy.

The role of brothers and sisters

Siblings in the home had a noticeable influence on the literacy climate there. The parents had noticed, for instance, that of the sixteen children with younger brothers and sisters, six of them (all girls) now read to their siblings or helped them to read:

'Something she has started to do is to listen to Ryan reading. It makes her feel responsible.'

'She'll sit and read to Luke.'

Parents mentioned other involvement with their younger siblings in pretend play, setting up situations such as school, police and shops; for example:

'She likes to play at teachers. She holds the book facing out like the teachers do. Jennie's picked it up from that.'

'He likes to play police. His uncle's a policeman. He says, "Right, Greg's going to prison", and he writes it all down.'

Some of the children enjoyed listening when their parent read to their younger brother or sister, and indeed two of the children were spurred on by the thought of their younger sibling competing with them; for example,

'As soon as he hears her say "can I read?", he wants to too.'

'There's only nineteen months between them. If he feels she's nearly caught up with him, he tries to keep ahead.'

As at the age of three, older siblings often influenced the children's literate behaviour in several ways. They provided a model; for instance,

'His sister had her homework every night. He tends to sit at the side of her and say, "I'll do my homework".'

'He makes little books. He draws a picture and writes underneath. He copies it off his brother.'

'She reads to herself most nights . . . she sees her sister doing that.'

They also gave access to resources that might not otherwise have been available, like computers and reference books. Some were involved in shared literacy activities such as reading books, writing together, and pretend play involving literacy, like playing at school; for instance,

'He likes to sit and play school with Leanne. She's always the teacher.'

'I play school with my sister. She teaches me all about me. She wrote down my friends, what I do at home, what I like best, telephone number and address, age. I fill it in and she marks it.'

Parents observed that some of the older siblings adopted a teacher stance, and deliberately helped with literacy learning; for instance,

'Her older sister writes words down for her from the dictionary and she finds them.'

'He sits for hours with her. He sits and listens to her. If she doesn't know a word he spells it out.'

'Ray learns me how to read his books and he reads some of mine and helps me.'

and some listened to their brother or sister read.

It has to be said that in some cases, having brothers and sisters increased distractions away from literacy. As Leanne, who had three older siblings, described,

'When my brother and sister put the telly on it puts me off. My mum can't hear what I'm saying and I have to start all over again. She makes sure the door's closed. We go in the room when my brother and sister are playing out and then it's nice and quiet.'

On the other hand, their influence was also positive, in that she also saw her siblings reading and writing while doing their homework, and on occasions they helped her with reading.

Several parents commented that the older siblings had increased the child's rate of progress, or stimulated an interest in literacy; for instance,

'Her sister's brought her on a lot.'

'It helps (his interest) when he sees Kerry read as well.'

From this we can see that in many different ways, being a sibling and having a sibling made a distinctive contribution to the literacy environment of the home.

Modelling adult uses of literacy in make-believe play

The majority of children showed that they had incorporated aspects of adult literacy practices into their pretend play. The most popular game was playing schools. This could involve other members of the family, or dolls and teddies:

'She likes to be the teacher. She sets us all work to do, like she does at school – what she's been doing, and she does some too.'

'He plays at school with his teddy bears and makes them little books.'

As well as the children's involvement in reading and writing for pretend school work, the children also liked to make up registers of children's names as part of their school play.

Other make-believe activities were playing at shops and post offices, families, which incorporated reading and writing, offices, and being a doctor, policeman, waitress, librarian, delivery man and club secretary. The examples that parents provided, that follow below, give an indication of the sort of play the children were engaged in:

'He plays at shops, usually a food shop, and uses tins and packets. He writes the amount down and things they are – writing different words down.'

'She plays families, grandma, mum and baby – and writes things down what she wants from the shop.'

'She has a toy stethoscope. She pretends to write prescriptions for her dolls.'

'With her toy cooker, she'll write things down, menus and things, and pretend to be a waitress.'

'He is a delivery man. He has a little thing with a clip on the top, and gives everybody a receipt.'

These examples give an indication of just how much the children had learned about literacy and its social applications, and how they were able to use play to practise and extend their own literacy competencies.

Intergenerational patterns of literacy

Although I did not specifically ask the parents if they had problems with literacy themselves, it became apparent that this was in fact the case for a small number of the parents, and they all had children who also had literacy difficulties. What follows are brief snapshots of three mothers' and children's engagement with literacy showing the literacy problems, and the adults' attempts to help the children.

Mark's mother, Jackie, recognised the importance of learning to read and write for her children's progress at school. Although she struggled with literacy herself at school, and had continuing difficulties as an adult, she wanted to provide books and writing materials for the children. But because these things were not part of her everyday life, she regarded them as 'special'. When I visited her, she showed me a collection of books, displayed on a high shelf in the best room. These were a collection of Ladybird books in sequence, 1a, 2a, 3a, etc., and a book of Bible stories given by the local church. The books had status for her, and were held in high regard, but they were not used. Mark (and his brother) had literacy difficulties through primary school, and Jackie herself said,

'I don't read for myself. I only read because of the children. I hate reading. There's lots of words I don't know so I skip them. I never read for pleasure.'

Denise was another parent who had literacy difficulties, commenting,

'I was like Bill (her son) at school, I had problems with reading and writing. I was in a special class at the comp.'

Like Jackie, Denise aimed to do her best for her children, but felt very uncertain how to go about helping them. When Bill was seven he was really struggling with his reading. Denise decided that the best way to help him was to read to him at bedtime, saying, 'we'll try, whether he'll listen or not'. She was reading to him from *He-Man*, a Ladybird book that had similar characters and story-lines to a television programme broadcast at the time. The book had the potential to be exciting, but the language in it was complex, and difficult for Denise to read aloud in a way that brought the story alive for Bill, because she felt he could only manage a little at any one reading session. She explained that she read, 'bits of it at a time – they're big books', and was intending to carry on 'til he can learn'.

Although she was clearly trying to help Bill, Denise was not giving Bill a particularly positive message about reading in the help she gave him. The text of the book was quite complex, and would probably have been difficult for a struggling reader to follow the story, especially if presented in little sections at a time.

Another parent, Jane, struggled with reading and writing as a child and as an adult. She said,

> 'I can't remember my parents reading with me. That's why I think I have problems with reading.'

Probably for that reason when her daughter Kirsty was little it did not occur to Jane to share books with her. The local health visitor was concerned when Kirsty was slow to learn to talk, and introduced Jane to the idea of their looking at books together.

At the time of talking with the parents I was very struck by the impression of *family* literacy difficulties in the situations I have just described, rather than problems that related to just the adult or the child on their own.

Parents engage in literacy practices and events

Parents reading to their children

When the children were seven, the practice of parents reading to their children still continued to be widespread in the families in the study. Only three of the children were not read to at home by their parents. Two of these children had reached a level of independence where they no longer wanted someone to do their reading for them. The initiative for parents to stop reading to them had come from the child as the parents were still willing to read to them:

> 'He may listen when I'm reading to his younger sister, but he wants to take over himself. He'll even read to his sister now.'

> 'I try to sit down and read to them both, but she gets up now, she's independent.'

The mother of the third child was also willing to read to her child, but he was resistant. She gave up trying to read to him because

'You couldn't sit him down properly. Perhaps there was too much pressure. He wouldn't sit, he'd kick the book.'

Children were usually read to mainly by their mother, although it is also true that nearly half the fathers read to the children. Other people who read to the children included their brothers and sisters, grandparents, aunts, babysitters and neighbours.

How often the children were read to varied. Most of the children read to everyday or most days were among the better readers. One child, Bill, was the struggling reader who was mentioned earlier. His mother Denise read to him regularly, every other night at bedtime because of the 'worry over him not reading', and did this whether he wanted to listen or not. By this stage, there were only two children having a regular bedtime story every night, but still over a third of the children had a bedtime story sometimes. A quarter of the children were read to once a week or less, so for these children, being read to was an intermittent rather than regular activity. Seven children were only read to for a few minutes at a time, while in contrast nine children were read to for half an hour or more, so there was a range of different practices associated with being read to for the children at home.

Parents were asked whose idea it usually was to read to the child. Often it was the child who took the initiative in asking for a reading session. For two-thirds of the children it was they who suggested reading, although their parents also sometimes suggested it. In fewer cases, it seemed to be the parent who took the initiative for reading at this stage. Two parents found it impossible to answer the question, because, they explained, 'It's what we've always done', and 'We just do it'.

One of these was Robin's mother who was aware of the value of reading to children, and had been the one parent to explain that she had consciously 'taught' reading by reading to him since he was tiny.

All this shows that being read to was still an important practice for seven-year-old children in a home and community setting.

What was read to the children

Parents were asked about what sorts of things were read to the children. Most of the children were usually read to from story books. Some of the children were read to from comics and annuals. Most of the non-fiction reading material shared with the children was in book form, including books about animals, football, trains, buses and motorbikes, a child's dictionary, a book of children's prayers and an atlas. Other sources included newspapers (read to two of the boys):

'I'll read him bits out of the *Daily Mirror* if I think they are of interest.'

'I read him anything to do with the local football team in the paper'

and the descriptions on football cards. A couple of girls were read to from mail order catalogues. Most of the children who were read to from non-fiction material also had stories read to them, but the boy read to from the *Daily Mirror* was read to not from story books but from reading scheme books. This suggests that for him, access to narrative forms at home was restricted.

These examples show how building up a composite picture of the range of materials used by individual children at home can throw light on their familiarity and experience, or lack of it, with some of the forms of literacy we often expect children to engage with at school. This may help to explain some of the differences of response by children to texts within a school setting. It also shows that children have experience with other forms of literacy which may well not be reflected in school at all, but which nonetheless contribute the children's actions and perceptions of themselves as users of literacy.

It was unusual for children to be read to from reading scheme books, but a few of them were, and two of the children were read to *only* from scheme books. Reading scheme books are often designed to help children learn to read by simplifying narrative structures and repeating commonly found words. They are not usually designed as books to read to children. In comparison to children being read to from other texts, children read to from reading schemes were listening to a restricted form of text, which limited the meanings that could be derived from the text. It was therefore probably not as rich an experience as being read to from other materials.

Parents teaching their children

Do parents feel they actively teach their children to read and write? The answer, in terms of the Elmswood study at least, is yes. Most of the parents said they were still teaching their seven-year-old child. When looking at *how* they did this, on the whole it was responding to and building on the child's own efforts. When teaching reading, a third of the parents helped children to sound out the letters in a word, sometimes emphasising the initial letter. They said, for example,

'If he's reading me a story and he's not sure of this word, such as bug, I say "buh-uh-guh" fast, so it sounds like bug.'

'Some words, you can sound them, like "duh" – "o" – "guh". What does that spell? What does it sound like? What does it begin with? What does it say? He knows that now.'

Children also gave examples of parents teaching them in this way, such as,

'My Mum helps by spelling the words out when I read them, like "tuh" – "oo", to.'

A number of parents simply told the child the word if they were stuck when reading, and some parents commented that if the child could not figure out the word using different methods, they would not leave them long before telling them the word:

'When we sit and she's reading and she gets stuck, I help her. I say, "Try and sound it out". Sometimes she can and sometimes she can't. I don't leave her struggling a long time, I tell her.'

A child explained,

'If I get stuck, they spell it out, and if I can't know what it is they tell me.'

Another strategy some parents used was to help their children by splitting up the unknown word, saying, for instance,

'If she gets stuck, I tell her to break it down, and see what words she could recognise within a word.'

'If he's stuck on a word, like "anything", I split it up for him. I cover up half the word, then the other half, then he can read it. We keep on and then go back to it.'

'He's got a lot of big words in his dinosaur books, like Diplodocus. I split it up into parts – he likes you to split them up.'

Children's comments included,

'If I don't know a word, mum and dad say "work it out" and if I can't read it they say half of it and then I get it.'

'When I get stuck on a word, mum says split it in two, and I do, and I get it wrong and then she tells me.'

Parents also adopted other teaching strategies such as reading the passage first and the child then reading it back, and helping the child not to run two sentences together. In addition, parents taught their child to recognise whole words, how to pronounce unknown words, checking that their reading made sense, and that their child had got the gist of the story. As well as supporting the children's own reading in these ways, several parents also used words written on individual cards (flashcards), both home-made and commercial, to help children learn new words, and one parent wrote sentences in which her child had to fill in the missing words.

Only three of the parents had been specifically asked to help by the school. For one, the request for parents to help in this way had been a general one to all parents of children attending this particular class. Two other parents had been asked to help with extra reading by the school (in these cases, it was because their child was having problems), practising reading cards with words on, and cards with words to learn and then put into sentences.

All this shows how widespread a variety of teaching strategies for helping with reading was for the majority of children within a home setting, and how this was usually done on the parents' own initiative without any structured consultation, support or other forms of interaction with the school. Family homes often provided in this way a rich resource where children could consolidate and in some cases extend literacy learning. Clearly school is not the only focus for this learning and development.

So far we have looked at the teaching of reading. Does a similar situation arise for children's writing within the home context? The answer again is yes, the majority of parents are involved. When teaching writing, over half the parents supplied words the children did not know how to spell. Examples given by parents included

'He writes short stories – a few lines. He starts writing and asks if he wants any help spelling words. I sound them out as he writes them.'

'Now if she gets stuck with spelling a word she comes and asks me. I spell it out and write it down.'

Children made comments like,

'The words I don't know, my mum writes on a piece of paper. I copy off them.'

'If I don't know how to spell summat Dad tells me how to spell it.'

Some of the parents gave help with the formation of letters, and the layout of words on the page, for instance,

'. . . more the neatness of it . . . like getting the letters the right way round, b's and d's. She gets those mixed up quite a lot.'

'I keep telling him to leave spaces between words. You can read what he does at school, but there's no spaces in between.'

One of the parents had been asked to help by the school. Kyle was asked to write rows of d's, b's and g's. Mrs S., his mother, helped Kyle make sure that the 'sticks' were 'going above and below the line'. This task was clearly a response to demands of the National Curriculum, for children to produce clear ascenders and descenders in their handwriting. The teacher had decided that it would help to enlist the support of parents to encourage children to practise this skill.

A few parents wrote out words for their child to copy, including children dictating the story and then copying it, and parents making up and writing out a story for the child to copy. Children also copied isolated words their parents had written for them. Only four parents talked of helping with the content of the writing. They described suggesting topics for stories, helping their child 'compile letters' to a friend, and helping their child write up regular projects undertaken at home, including, for example, one about gymnastics.

A few parents were wary of their intervention possibly undermining their child's efforts, saying, for example,

'It's a difficult thing to help with other than spelling. I don't want to appear too critical. I tell her letters – she'll ask me how to spell something. Her grandparents tend to be a bit critical . . . "you have to write on the line".'

'I don't criticise too much, she tends to take it personally.'

'If she hasn't done something right and I try and show her I put her off sometimes. I think I'm a bit hard – I haven't got a lot of patience.'

Most parents felt actively involved in literacy teaching. There were only three parents who said they did not teach reading, and only six who said they did not teach writing at this stage. The reasons given by the parents not teaching reading varied. One child did not want his parent to help, 'he won't let me help at the moment', and earlier when his parent had tried to teach him to read some words 'he didn't want to know'. The mother of a second child said he did not read out loud 'because he can't'. She was unsure how she could help:

'I don't know where to start with him. He doesn't have a lot of interest, and now I lose my temper quick.'

The third child was the only one in the study for whom English was a second language. Her mother did not read English. She said,

'Other parents can read to their children, but I can't. I can't teach her.'

These three parents were really stuck, and were obviously unsure about what they could contribute. While they were clearly in a minority, they show that parents can be uncertain, and may well have welcomed some support from professionals.

In terms of teaching writing, two of the children who were not taught to read at home (both amongst the poorest in literacy in the sample) were not taught to write either. The parents' reasons, not knowing how to help, and not feeling able to help, were the same as for not teaching children to read. The other children not taught to write by their parents had, however, had their help in the past. Now their parents felt their child did not really need or want help at this time. As one parent explained,

'You can read what he's writing now.'

Another felt more structure would give her a clearer idea of how to help:

'He's hoping for homework from the juniors. That way you can help him more.'

A few of the children did not seem to express a need for help at this stage. Those parents who were unclear what to do or unsure how to help did not seem to have advice or support to help them with this. However, from these many examples it becomes clear just how involved the majority of parents were in actively helping their own children with literacy. For a minority, more support could well have been beneficial.

Literacy learning in day-to-day activities

As we have seen, when parents were asked whether they *taught* their child to read and write, most of those who said yes emphasised the *form* of the activity rather than the *content*. However, when talking more generally with parents a different picture emerged. It turned out that parents were indeed involved in a range of activities which taught the children about the content and purpose of literacy, but these often occurred as an integral part of a more general activity. Much of this teaching and learning was effectively 'invisible' in that it occurred so naturally and was so much a part of day-to-day living, that it could go unnoticed. But even so all but four parents were able to describe a variety of situations connected with family life in which literacy learning took place. As they talked, some parents had a sense of just how much they were actually doing. As one said,

'I suppose until you think about it you don't know how much you do.'

Teaching and learning are framed differently at home and at school. Unlike teachers, who specifically plan to teach children about literacy, parents often have a less consciously intentional approach. Many parents were uneasy with the term 'teach' to describe what they were doing with their children. They commented, for instance,

'Not so much teach him. We'd look at books. He'd say, "What does that say?" I think that's part of learning.'

'Teaching, maybe I was, unconsciously, by looking at books.'

'I didn't sit down and teach "ah" – "buh" – "cuh". I did it gradually, at his own pace.'

'I wouldn't really call it "teaching her to read".'

'I wouldn't say I'd sit her down and say, we'll read now.'

'We encourage him all we could – pointing words out. Teach is not the right word. If we're doing everyday things, we'd point words out, such as on a game.'

The children whose parents, when they had thought about it, could still not supply examples of literacy activities occurring in day-to-day life, were amongst the children with literacy difficulties at age seven. It may well be that some measure of literacy activity at home as an ordinary part of daily activities is helpful to children as they learn about literacy. However, the main message of the study was that parents of the majority of the children were able to provide numerous examples of everyday literacy events and practices through which children had direct experience of the purposes for literacy within a home and community setting.

By way of illustration, we will now look at examples of the sorts of day-to-day activities which the parents recognised as including literacy. At home, parents mentioned writing letters, cards and invitations together, writing shopping lists, doing crosswords and wordsearches together (including Ricky's family where Ricky and his mother sent off the results of a wordsearch to a newspaper, and actually won tickets to Blackpool), reading items together from the television, reading the back of cereal packets and sending off for things, reading recipes together for baking, and selecting a holiday destination from brochures. Two of the parents explicitly aimed to show their children how you could use reading to gain information. They commented,

'I teach Sarah she can get more information by using reading, like looking in a catalogue for something she wants like a sleeping bag, or looking for a television programme – that it's an information giving thing.'

'If I came across anything like tadpoles at nursery, or Martin's been on a walk collecting conkers, we'll look it up in the encyclopaedia.'

In some cases, the parents doing work at home gave children the idea for certain literacy activities; for example, one parent mentioned doing the books for a family business, and her child wanted to be involved:

'She'd want to do the same. She says, "Oh, I'll do a letter mummy".'

Another two parents studied and wrote at home:

'Sometimes if I'm doing my work she'll sit alongside me, but she's writing independently.'

'If Mick's sat at the table drawing or writing, he'll want to join in with him.'

Some of the parents mentioned activities outside the home as opportunities for literacy learning, such as going on journeys and travelling generally. For instance, they commented,

'She asks what the signs say on the road.'

'We work out train and bus timetables. Where do we want to get to next? Where are we? How do we get there?'

'We read things on buses. When we go out for the day, they pick out road signs – they have to look out for road signs.'

'When we're on our way to the seaside, we see who can spot the name first, and how far it is.'

A number of parents described occasions when they were involved in everyday activities in their local community as times when they incorporated literacy learning into what they did with their child; for example:

'If we're shopping we look at the guide telling you where all the shops are.'

'When we're in the supermarket he knows which is soap powder and Comfort and margarine and that.'

'We write a list for Tesco. I push the trolley and they get things for me.'

'I point things out like car park, the signpost for the toilets. . . .'

'On Monday we went for a walk and there was a notice saying private. I asked her, "What do you think it says?" She started to say p-r- . . . I told her it was private, and what it meant.'

'We look at the hymn book and sing hymns at church.'

Several parents gave examples of special outings and going on holiday as times that gave rise to literacy related to the activity, such as going to local places of interest, going to a zoo or farm, and going on holiday:

'Yesterday we went on a farm trail. There were blackboards above each different animal, "My name is Matilda. My babies were born on such and such". There were labels like a farm trail – to follow the arrows.'

'We went to visit (a local historic house). If you take them to places like this they understand better – there's things to read in all the rooms.'

'When we went to France, she wanted me to write things down in English and French.'

'We went to London for her birthday. We went to the tube and she was wanting to know all the different stops.'

Sam's family went on holiday to Butlins, and while he was there Sam wrote a postcard to the teacher and children at school. It was later pinned on the class notice board, and was still there on his return, so he could see that it had been received and valued.

Because these types of activity are sometimes hard for parents to disentangle from the day-to-day business of everyday life, there is likely to have been under-reporting of what was happening with the parents and children. However, these examples give a flavour of the types of home and family-based activities involving literacy that parents and children engaged in together, giving a rich and contextualised setting in which to learn some of the lessons about what it is to be literate.

Summary

What were the literacy environments of children at home, at age seven?

All the children in the Elmswood study continued to have a range of experiences of literacy at home up to age seven. In many cases these were extensive, but there remained a minority for whom such events were an infrequent occurrence. Literacy at home was often different from school literacy and literacy for children with difficulties was often different from literacy experiences of other children.

Resources and opportunities for literacy

All but one child had books bought for them at this stage. School had had an impact on book buying through bookclubs and annual book fairs. A number of parents bought books from local shops, or from shops in town, while a minority bought most books from bookshops. All children owned some books of their own. Very few had no more than a dozen, and the majority had more than fifty books each. More children were library members than at the pre-nursery stage. Again children who owned most books were most likely to be library members, widening their access to books at home.

The majority of children had favourite books. The types of book they chose varied, and included children's novels, picture story books, popular children's fiction many with characters from television programmes or films, fairy tales and rhymes, non-fiction books (chosen by boys), and a reading scheme book (a favourite of a child with reading difficulties). A few children were critical of the reading material from school and preferred what they read at home.

All children had a range of resources for drawing and writing, in some cases wider than others, but the opportunity was available to all.

Most parents provided other resources for literacy, including commercially produced books, toy computers, flashcards, story tapes, typewriters and games. A few parents voiced criticism of commercially produced materials aimed at teaching reading and writing, because they did not hold their child's interest. Nearly three-quarters of the children had access to a computer at home, and most parents thought their child had learned useful literacy skills in their interactions with the keyboard and the software.

Literacy models

Only a few children were unable to provide examples of seeing someone reading or writing at home. Parents gave examples of the way older siblings provided literacy models for the children. Children showed how they had noticed adults' uses of literacy in their make-believe play.

Parents' interactions with literacy activities with their children

Almost all children still had books read to them by their parents at this stage. Boys were the most likely to share non-fiction. Whilst some children were read to from a wide range of reading material, including both fiction and non-fiction, for others, their reading matter was more restricted.

The few parents who did not teach their child reading or writing at home said this was because they felt the child did not want them to help, they felt they did not know how to help or that they were unable to help. A very small number of parents had been asked to help their child by the school. A couple of children, taught neither reading nor writing at home, were amongst the poorest in literacy amongst the group.

In describing their 'teaching' of reading and writing parents commented mainly about the form of the activity. They were, however, also concerned with the content and purpose of literacy, which became apparent as they described literacy which occurred as part of ordinary everyday activities. Almost all parents were able to provide examples. Those that could not had children who were amongst the children having problems with literacy.

While this chapter has focused mainly on the interactions of parents and children together, in the next chapter we look in greater detail at the nature of interactions between parents and teachers.

7

Home–School Relations and Children's Literacy

We have explored in some depth the literacy environments of the children's homes. But what happens at the interface with schools? In this chapter I survey various aspects of home–school relations, ranging from a detailed look at some of the specific ways that parents and teachers work together to help the children, to more general enquiries about how they relate with one another. The reason for doing this is to explore what this might mean for children's literacy.

Children reading to parents from school books

Since a number of key research projects in the 1970s and 1980s showed the possibilities and the benefits of children reading to their parents from books used in school (for example, Tizard, Schofield and Hewison, 1982, Griffiths and Hamilton, 1984, Hannon, 1987), it has become a fairly widespread aspect of practice in many primary schools for children to take books home from school. And so it was within all eight of the schools that the children went to in the Elmswood study when the children were seven. I asked all the parents if their child brought reading books home, and it was only two of the forty-two parents who said their child did not bring a school book to read to someone at home. Indeed many of the children brought their books home frequently, with ten of the children taking books home most days or even every day, and fourteen taking books home two or three times a week, although there were also eighteen children who took them home once a week or less. Reading books were sent home from all the schools. There was one school where every child was asked to take their book home each day.

The parents said that all the children who took a reading book home read it aloud to someone at home at least sometimes, except for one child who used to, but since the age of about six could read on her own. Her mother said, 'She reads to herself now.' The parents reported that all children read aloud most frequently to their mothers. About a third of the children also read to their fathers. Children also read regularly to older siblings, and to grandparents, including Laura who, at age seven, explained,

> 'When I go out with my grandma she can't see very well, so I have to read the letters for her and postcodes.'

The children also read to other relatives, to family visitors and to friends.

The parents were asked how often the children read out loud to others at home. What they said is summarised in Table 5. What we see is that the children tended to read to others at home a great deal. Parents of nearly half the children said they read out loud either daily or most days, and a further third read out loud two or three times a week. There were only six children who brought their school book home and only read to others once a week or less, but these were *not* the weakest readers. By the age of seven, reading out loud may not be the most helpful method for those children already reading well. However, there were two parents who said that their child (both of them weak readers) never read out loud at home *at all*, which suggests that lack of such practice at home may be disadvantageous.

Having talked with the parents, I also asked the children, when I spent time talking with them about literacy, whether they had taken a school book home on the previous night. This was to gauge the extent to which this was regular common practice. Over a third of the children had done

Table 5 How often children read to others at home at age seven

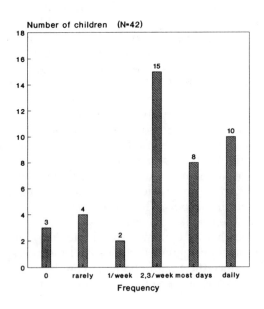

so. This gives the impression that taking reading books home was more firmly embedded in school practice than was implied by an earlier, similar survey, conducted by Hannon and Cuckle (1984), where they found that while children were allowed to take their books home, not many had actually done so on the particular occasion when they were asked about it.

What's expected of parents?

I explored with parents how far they felt they knew what was expected of them when a school reading book did come home, and their child read aloud to them. The majority said that they felt confident they had an idea, and made comments like,

'I sit and listen to her read and try to help her with words she doesn't know.'

However, there were also many parents who felt that they had to make assumptions, making comments such as,

'I think we're expected to read to her and her to read back to us, and put her right on her mistakes. I just assume that – we've never been asked to do that.'

'We sit and let her read. If she gets stuck on any words we help her with them, but we try to get her to work it out. She would usually. I can't remember having been told. In earlier stages, if she had difficulties, she had a card in her book, "let Suzanne do such and such". It helped.'

'Nothing's said, but I'm happy about what I'm doing.'

While the majority of parents were able to use their initiative and felt reasonably confident in the way they supported their child's school-initiated reading, a sizeable proportion of parents still felt unclear. It was often difficult to bridge the information gap between parents and schools for some of the parents, particularly those who could most benefit from such information, and this is something that will be discussed further in Chapter 10.

Half the parents were happy with how often their child brought their book from school. The flexibility of the system, whereby children and parents could choose when to take books home, was generally welcomed; for instance, parents said,

'It's just right – it's left to you.'

'I think they ought to leave it to the individual. If the reading books come home too much, you could pressurise them (the children).'

'You can set the pace. The reading books are always available to come home. The relaxed atmosphere makes it much easier.'

While these parents seemed happy to 'set the pace', other parents were less happy about the arrangements. They implied that they would have liked a more proactive approach by the school. More than a third of parents thought that their child did not bring reading books home often enough, and made comments like,

'I don't think they're encouraged enough. I'm waiting in the car, I don't always go in.'

'It's not pushed enough at school.'

It seems that a flexible approach was creating gaps in the system. But a more rigid policy can have its problems too. The parent whose child attended the only school where books were systematically sent home every night thought her child brought books home too frequently. His mother commented,

'I think every night is a bit much. It feels as if they've got to do it. Sometimes you feel you don't want to do it. If you push Adam to do something, he'll not do it.'

I think the message here is that schools need to be clear about their policy on sending reading books home, consistently communicate their plans and the rationale for them to parents, and ensure that *all* children involved have similar opportunities to be part of whatever scheme is adopted.

Beyond school readers

Children did not just read to others from their school reading books at home, although this was not recorded in any way. In fact it turned out that the majority of the children read to their parents from a wide range of reading material. Many of the children were reading to parents from their own books at home. Other books children read from were library books, or their brothers' and sisters' books. Children also read to their parents from newspapers, to find out football results, what was on television, and the headlines, reading the 'large print'. Some parents commented on their children reading from the television, including from Oracle, and others noticed their child's reading from print in the environment, for example,

'He reads signs when we're going round, like, "dogs must be on a lead".'

Another parent gave an example from the kitchen:

'He'll tell you what you're supposed to be doing, like instructions for a cake mixture.'

Children also read to their parents from comics, annuals and football programmes and from magazines, including a television listing magazine.

It was noticeable that at home the majority of the children were reading to others from materials written in a range of different genres, which were often produced explicitly to inform or entertain, and which gave the children reasons to engage with the materials other than simply for reading practice. This experience was not, however, explicitly recognised at school.

Parental involvement in school

Parents were asked if they had some involvement within school, working with their own child during school time, working with groups of children, or helping in some other way. A high proportion, half the parents, said that they had had some involvement. For most of them this was through attending a Reading Workshop at one of the schools in the study, which was designed for parents to work alongside their own child in school on reading and reading-based games. Of those parents who did not attend but had children going to the school, four parents were at work or did not have time to attend, one of the parents used to go, but was no longer able to because she had a young toddler to look after, and another had been in the past. There were also three parents who said they did not want to go. Parents mentioned two other forms of parental involvement in school – helping out in class, and attending school lessons. Three parents helped out in class, including helping with children's reading and writing, on a regular basis. Two of these parents had previously worked professionally but were currently based at home looking after their children. The third helped to run a local parent and toddler group. All said they enjoyed work in the classroom and felt confident in the school setting. As one of them described it, 'it's like a second home up there.'

One mother had taken the opportunity offered to sit in on a lesson in school, and had found it helpful. Three other parents said they could not become involved at school because of work commitments and having other children under five. In two of the schools that children in the Elmswood study attended at seven, no such opportunities were provided. One parent contrasted her perceptions of her child's current school with her earlier experience of another school, where parents could bring their child into the classrooms and collect them from there:

> 'You don't go into the school. In the last school, you saw your teachers every day, and if you'd got any comments, you could just tell them. There you're not allowed to go in.'

This clearly reduced the possibilities of parental contact with teachers on a day-to-day basis, and reduced the opportunities for discussion and exchange of information. The second parent described how parental involvement at her child's school was on a 'social basis' and 'fundraising', although 'one or two key figures . . . were able to go in and help'.

The divergent experiences of the parents provide us with a reflection of parents' perceptions of ways in which schools respond to the involvement of parents in literacy within school.

Behind closed doors?

Only a minority of parents felt they knew how reading and writing were taught in school, and uncertainty was the norm. Two-thirds of the parents said they did not know how writing was taught, and slightly fewer how reading was taught. Indeed, well over half of the parents were unsure about the teaching of both reading and writing. More information would have been welcomed; for instance, parents made comments like,

'He did a lot of letters the wrong way round. I asked his teacher about it . . . You don't really find out from school about how they teach reading and writing . . . You don't always like to bother them, you think they've enough on with all the children.'

'I think parents ought to be a lot more involved. I think parents should be told a lot more exactly how they teach them, then they could help them a lot better at home.'

'They don't tell us about what our kids are doing. If they'd tell us more, we'd be able to help them better.'

Those parents who themselves initiated contact with teachers, or chose to spend time in school at some time during the week, were the group of parents with the most knowledge about what their children were being taught in school.

Contact about literacy between parents and teachers

Parents were asked whether they talked with their child's teacher specifically about reading and writing, in addition to twice-yearly parent–teacher consultations. The majority of parents did talk with the teacher about literacy at other times. Of those that did not, most said they were not involved in any way at school. It appeared that lack of regular contact within school lessened the likelihood of a dialogue between parents and teachers concerning children's literacy. Such dialogue between parents and teachers is important for children's literacy development, since increased contacts have been shown to have positive consequences for children's literacy performance (see, for instance, Iverson, Brownlee and Walberg, 1981, Snow *et al.*, 1991). On the whole, teachers tended to let parents take the initiative in talking about literacy (apart from formal consultations). As a result, some parents received a great deal more information than others. Some of the parents who might have benefited from information did not receive it. Parents taking the initiative has also been reported in a number of earlier studies which looked at parent–staff consultation in relation to preschool education (for example, Tizard, Mortimore and Burchell, 1981, Blatchford, Battle and Mays, 1982). Typical comments from those parents who did talk with the teachers concerned their need to ask in order to find out any information:

'If I've got any questions, I ask.'

'If it weren't for parents' day I don't think we'd really get to know much – unless you ask, which I do.'

This form of contact relies on a level of confidence and some understanding of literacy learning on the part of the parents.

Teachers too reported that talk was usually initiated by parents, and often in response to problems perceived by the parent; for instance,

'If mum has the least little thing, she wants to be there to help and support. She's asked for advice, and done it.'

'She asked me why he wasn't reading. . . .'

'When we have a chat, she asks about her handwriting.'

Those parents who did not have contact with the teachers concerning literacy expected that they would be told if there were any problems:

'They invite you to go in if you've a problem. I don't seem to, so I don't seem to bother them.'

'I haven't spoken to the teacher (about reading or writing) an awful lot. Probably if they had been worried they'd have told me.'

Similarly teachers felt there was less to say if there were no immediate problems. One parent commented,

'I couldn't go to the open day. His teacher wasn't worried about his work, so rightly or wrongly she thought it didn't matter that I missed it.'

Communication between parents and teachers tended to occur with regular contact. In this way, a particular group of parents, often those who had the most confidence and knowledge about literacy in the first place, had the most frequent discussions about literacy with the teachers in school. A more consistent flow of communication with all parents could help with parents' confidence, help children to be more supported, and also alert teachers to some of the literacy learning occurring at home which may otherwise have been overlooked.

Encouragement to parents

I wondered whether parents felt they had had encouragement from school for reading and writing with their child. Five parents made comments that showed they felt very positive about how much they were encouraged by school, saying, for instance,

'Yes, I should say so. If you've got time, they have. There's all sorts. You can go in anytime and read with your child.'

'Yes. There's the folders. We didn't used to take reading books home when we were at school. There's Reading Workshop.'

These five parents were all amongst those who had regular contact with the school. Three helped out in class, one was a school parent governor, and one attended a Reading Workshop in school regularly. There was also a large number of other parents who felt they had been encouraged in some way by school, for instance through school books coming home, being invited to literacy activities in school, or talking with their child's teacher. One parent said she felt encouraged once she had taken the initiative to go and ask how her child was getting on with his reading. The teacher then started sending additional reading material home in response to this. This provides another example of dialogue between parent and teacher occurring as a result of the parent taking the initiative. One working parent commented that the school arranged events and encouraged parents to help with their children's literacy in school, but that she personally had not been able to attend.

While many parents felt they had been given explicit encouragement from school for reading and writing with their children, over a third did not feel encouraged in this way. Comments made showed a certain reluctance on the part of teachers and parents to take up one another's time, for instance,

> 'You don't always like to bother them (the teachers). You think they've enough on with all the children.'

> 'No . . . I don't know if it's because they've not been worried about her.'

> 'I think they let me get on with it.'

This limited opportunities for teachers to convey encouragement to parents, and for recognition on the part of both teachers and parents of what one another was doing.

Different literacies?

Did parents feel that there were essential differences between the literacy learning of their child at home and at school? When I asked parents about this, some did not feel there were. Five parents were unable to comment because of lack of knowledge about what their child did at school. Of the comments that were made, the majority were about *positive* aspects of literacy that *home* had to offer. Parents spoke, for instance, of their child's free choice of activities, and that they were self-motivated at home. They mentioned children being able to do things that fitted in naturally with daily life and arose from, 'things that happen in and around the family'. These included such activities as reading selections from the paper, writing about visiting a relative, or using a dictionary. Other parents felt the children encountered less distractions at home than in a busy classroom. Two parents commented that children had access to books they could select for themselves. As one of them said,

'I think she's limited at school, with her school books. Here, she can start with a book with only a few words in and then get a book with lots of words. In the books she brings home, there's only just one word added. She could do with something a bit more grown up.'

Another parent mentioned the sustained support parents could offer for reading experiences at home:

'At home, she's always got somebody to read to her. It can be one-to-one. The teacher has to spread herself a long way with twenty-six children in the class.'

There were also five parents who gave examples where they felt school could offer more than home. Three of them thought their child had a wider range of literacy experiences at school, one said her child would attempt spelling at school but not at home, and one would write stories rather than copy write at school but not at home.

In summary, many parents felt positive about the contribution of literacy at home and were aware that there were distinct differences in the types of literacy children encountered at home and at school.

Teachers had many positive things to say about the importance of parents' input into the children's literacy learning, mentioning, for example, their help with language development, their acting as literacy role models, their ability to share an enjoyment of books, to point out print to the children, and to supply them with material resources and experiences. At the level of the individual parents the teachers' information was more limited. When teachers were asked about the possible differences between home and school literacy, like some of the parents, teachers of ten children were unable to comment because they did not feel they knew enough about what happened at home in terms of literacy. In only just under a third of the families did teachers feel that parents were engaging in literacy practices with their child, to any appreciable extent, in a similar way to the school. And in only one instance did a teacher feel that home was offering something positive in addition to what the school provided. This was a child with an older sibling, where family provision catered for a 'more mature interest level than school'. On the whole, then, teachers seemed to be rather unclear about what many of the children's homes offered as literacy learning environments.

The teachers were also asked specifically about the level of support they felt parents gave to the children's reading and writing. In two cases, teachers thought the home provided little support, and for three other families, teachers thought there was no support for writing. In five families the teachers felt they did not know enough to comment. They estimated only a little support was offered by about a quarter of the parents, and some support from about a third of the parents. It was only about a third of families which, in teachers' estimation, offered children a great deal of support for literacy.

To sum up then, the Elmswood study demonstrates that virtually all parents help their children in some way with literacy. Some parents do this more consciously than others, and some have more confidence about what they are doing than others. However, it seems that the schools tended to have limited knowledge about what parents do with their children at home on literacy. Increased communication might have provided a clearer picture, and enhanced mutual understanding about the literacy learning which children engaged with in the different settings of home and school.

Summary of the nature of home–school relations

The level of communication parents had with school varied. Some parents had considerable contact with their child's teacher, while other parents with children in the same class had little contact. Many of the parents were confused about how to support their child's literacy learning.

Children from all eight schools in the study were able to take school books home. Only a couple of the children did not do so. The majority of children read out loud from a wider range of materials than that supplied by the school, including from newspapers, comics and annuals, the television and print in the environment. These gave children other reasons to read than simply for practice. Only two of the children never read out loud at home at all, and they were both weak readers. For the other children there was variation in how often they read to their parents, but those reading out loud least often were not necessarily the weakest readers.

The children were asked whether they had taken a reading book home from school on the previous night, and over a third of the children had done so. Many parents were not sure of what was expected of them when their child brought home a reading book, and made their own assumptions. Half the parents were happy with how often the children brought home a reading book, but more than a third thought the books did not come home often enough. However, the parent of the child in the only school where books were sent home every night thought that this was too frequent.

Half the parents were involved in some way within the school. Some parents were unable to become involved because of work and other commitments.

Most parents did not know how reading or writing was taught in school, and most would have liked more information. The parents with the most knowledge included those who initiated contact with the teachers, or who elected to spend some time in school. Regular contact increased the likelihood of parent and teacher discussions. Teachers tended to wait for parents to take the initiative in talking about their child's literacy.

Where parents made comments about differences between literacy learning at home and school most expressed positive opinions about the contribution of the home. Teachers tended to be rather less positive about what home had to offer. The teachers did not know about the reading and writing activities at home for the majority of children in their class. While most of the parents said they helped with literacy at home, teachers' estimations were that only about a third of parents were offering their children a great deal of support for literacy. The findings of the Elmswood study, then, suggest there is scope for increasing and enhancing the communication of parents and teachers over literacy, for the benefit of children's literacy development.

In the next chapter, we start to explore some of the factors that influence the parents' role in relation to supporting their children's literacy learning.

8

Influences on the Parents' Role

In Chapters 5 and 6 I referred to the framework, outlined in Appendix 1, for looking at the role of parents in their children's literacy development. The framework indicates factors which may influence how and why parents **provide resources, act as literacy models, and engage with their children on literacy practices and events**. The parents' role in literacy involves attitudes and ideas that have been built up within a socio-cultural context over time, as a subtle result of a whole range of pre-dispositions and external circumstances. Some of these may therefore be hard to access. Some of the more obvious factors which influence the role of parents in their children's literacy development will be discussed here.

Ideas on reading to children

I wondered how widespread the practice of parents reading to their children was, once the children were aged seven. In fact, all but three of the parents were still reading to their children at this stage. When I asked them how long they anticipated doing this for, every parent responded that they would carry on as long as their child wanted it or needed it. They said their prompt to stop reading would be the child being able to read proficiently on their own, or saying they did not want to be read to any more. Typical comments included

> 'I think we'll go on reading 'til she gets to the age where she can do it herself with no problems. Once she can read herself, she'll want to do it herself.'

> 'Probably when she gets fed up she'll tell us.'

> 'I will read as long as he wants me to.'

> '(I'll read to him) until he can read a book himself.'

> 'That's up to her. I'll always encourage it.'

Here we have an indication of how committed the parents were to supporting their children's reading, by providing props and encouragement until such a time as their children would no longer need it.

Reasons for sharing books

Many of the parents were sharing books with their children, but could they articulate their reasons for doing this? Of those parents who looked at books with their seven-year-old children, the majority offered positive explanations of why they shared books. They mentioned helping their children learn, giving them experience and information, encouraging them with reading, doing it for enjoyment and relaxation, and as a way of spending time together. Two parents said they shared books because their child asked them to. Of those parents offering less positive explanations, two shared books but could not explain why, and one did so because she was worried about her child not reading. Two parents of failing readers had a very narrow view of the purpose of sharing books with their child. Both interacted with their child on labelling and naming pictures rather than exploring narrative, and were prescriptive in the way this was done. They explained,

'He spots pictures in it (i.e. the book). "Here is a tree. Here is Jane in a tree. Here is a toyshop. Peter is in a toyshop." He can see it in the picture. I have to give him something simple.'

'To tell her what's happening in the picture. She likes to tell me what's happening.'

Both these parents were limiting their children's interactions with books. In their efforts to help they had over-simplified the task of 'reading', and in so doing, made it potentially harder for their children to learn effectively the lessons that books can teach. Shirley Brice Heath (1983) and Fitzgerald, Spiegel and Cunningham (1991) also found similar examples in their research.

The benefits of literacy

Why is literacy necessary? I was interested to know whether parents thought there were benefits for their children from learning to read and write. Most parents could articulate a number of reasons, including to gain knowledge, to communicate, to find one's way about and interact with print in the world, and for pleasure. A few parents mentioned how problematic life could be without literacy skills, saying, for instance,

'When they go out they can do their shopping. I don't know how they go on when they can't read and write.'

'Round here I've seen a lot of children who are illiterate. They just hang around, and it's an awful waste.'

'It's not until you go to a foreign country or pick up a book in a language you can't read, and you realise this is how it feels to people who can't read.'

A minority of parents did not express such views. One parent gave the benefit simply as 'practice', and another said, 'I think they learn to enjoy school more when they can see what everyone else is doing'. Five other parents said they did not know what benefits in literacy there were for their children. So while the benefits of literacy were apparent to the majority of parents, this was not the case for a small minority, who may have had very restricted views of the purposes of literacy.

Advice

Do parents feel they receive much advice about the teaching of literacy? When the children in the study were aged three, I asked their parents whether they had had any advice about children learning to read and write. On the whole they said that they had not. Most of the ideas parents had about reading and writing development seemed to come from their own observations, probably informed by their memories of literacy at school and at home, making comments such as, 'I do what my mum and dad did with us' or 'I can only teach him what I know myself'.

A number of parents said they were unsure about what they should be doing about teaching reading and writing to their child. One parent, for instance, spelled out what she saw as a need for advice at this stage:

'It's knowing what to do and how to approach it and how much to do at a time. I'm sure a lot of parents don't have confidence, and would like someone to say whether they're doing it right'.

When parents were asked if they were confused about whether to use 'ah', 'buh', 'cuh', or 'aye', 'bee', 'cee' with their children, nearly half the parents admitted they were confused; for example, one parent said,

'I don't know whether to teach him 'es, aye, em' or 'suh, ah, muh'. I don't know how they go on at school. I didn't want to learn him wrong.'

These uncertainties could undermine parents' confidence, and point to the need to provide parents *early* with information about aspects of literacy.

On the other hand, ten parents said that they had had advice about literacy. A few parents had been given advice by teachers for their older children, and had generalised from this. One of the parents had been advised not to help with reading and writing at home as this could lead to confusion, and another was told that her daughter, Carrie, who was not yet reading, would do so 'when she's ready'. This left Carrie's mother even more unclear than before. She explained, 'if they don't send any-thing home, you don't know what stage they're at' (this was at a school where reading and writing were not sent home). A couple of parents mentioned receiving advice from relatives who were in fact primary school teachers, and another couple of parents were advised to start their children reading early by their own mothers (one as a result of seeing a television programme about reading). One of the parents had been ad-vised by the local health visitor to get some books and sit and read with her because her child had delayed speech development. A further parent, while saying she had not received advice, had taken the prompt to read to her child when a relative gave him a book just before his first birthday:

> 'Before he was one I never dreamt of reading to him, but when my auntie gave him a book, it set us off.'

This demonstrates the impact such a 'suggestion' can have. We live within such complex environments, in which we deal with many such implicit and explicit messages about literacy. Advice can be given consciously, and taken on board or rejected, but it can also be absorbed more subtly, as with the example of a book as a present for a baby.

By the time the children were aged seven, again most parents said they used their own experience and ideas to inform how they interacted with their child on literacy. As one parent expressed it,

> 'What I know is because I've used my own initiative. I've always thought it was important that they should read and write.'

Information about children's literacy

What about feeling informed about children's literacy? In the Elmswood study over half the parents felt that most of the information they had received about how children learn to read and write came through their children, their family and friends, magazines, newspapers and television. Most frequently mentioned was what parents learned from children showing them what they were doing and telling them about literacy at school. For other parents, their primary source of information was from members of their family, and from other parents, saying, for instance, 'I ask my mum' or 'probably within the family, with my other sisters having older children'.

Ten parents gleaned information on literacy from books which set out to explain children's early reading and writing and five parents said they had picked up information about literacy from magazines. Eight parents mentioned information from television, both from documentary programmes such as *Help your child to read* and *40 minutes*, and from children's television programmes with a literacy content, such as *Sesame Street*. Two parents could not suggest sources of information on literacy because they felt they did not know about it.

All this shows that many parents felt that information about literacy came principally from informal channels of communication.

Parents' expectations

The majority of parents said that they expected to enjoy reading, and indeed read for pleasure themselves. All but three of the parents who did not read for pleasure had children with some problems with reading or who did not enjoy reading much. When parents were asked about their literacy expectations for their children, the only five parents who did not think their child would make much use of reading and writing in the future did not read for pleasure themselves. One child was described as being 'not academic, more technical'. For him, reading and writing were described as being a

> 'necessary evil. I don't think he'll ever gain pleasure from it. He finds it boring'.

Another parent also thought it was not likely that her child would be much involved in literacy later because,

> 'at the moment he doesn't seem all that interested.'

Two parents thought their children would not use much literacy later, and one revealed a very narrow view of the purpose of literacy:

> 'Only at school. I'll keep on with his reading. I'd like him to go through the books I've bought him, otherwise it would be a waste of money.'

These views provide an example of the interrelationship of parent and child perspectives. Expectations and attitudes towards literacy often develop at a family, rather than solely at an individual, level. Understanding the parents' stance towards literacy can help with an understanding of the child's literacy perspective.

Parents' experiences of family literacy

Socio-cultural practices are often passed on from one generation to the other, literacy practices being one of them. I was therefore interested in the parents' own childhood experiences of literacy, and the ways these were confirmed or altered in the way the parents interacted with their children. While all the children in the study were helped with literacy in some way by their parents, and the majority were read to, only half the parents recollected having had these experiences themselves as children. When they did, this was often to a lesser extent. Parents commented, for instance,

> 'My mother (read to me). Not like we do it with them, not to the same extent. When I was at school, parents weren't consulted. If anybody's mother came up to school it was an event.'

> 'Not as much as we do. I don't think they did at that time.'

Parents provided a range of examples of the literacy practices they were involved in with parents and other family members, such as,

> 'I was read to a lot, including at bedtime.'

> 'I suppose my mum read to me, but not writing. I can remember writing stories with my grandparents every weekend. My grandfather gave encouragement with story writing. He pointed things out – this could be better, and he would buy a new exercise book and pencil.'

'Yes, with my mother. She used to sit hours. She had ten kids and she'd leave her work and sit with us. My mother used to like to read and write. I think that's where I get it from.'

'I used to read a lot with my father. We read newspapers back and front. Mum was the one who played games to do with reading.'

'Grandad looked at Rupert books with me. I can remember when I was three, the books had things to do in them. My grandfather made a cage out of straws for me out of my Rupert book.'

'Yes, with my dad more than my mum, and three older sisters. They used to read a lot.'

Many of the children in the Elmswood study had similar experiences at home.

But in contrast, there were many parents who could not remember any involvement in literacy practices. Where parents suggested explanations, these were that large families implied lack of time, and made interaction with individual children difficult (two families had seven children, one nine, and one eleven; none of the children in the study were from such large families), and parents being busy at work.

Parents were not asked whether they had literacy difficulties themselves, but a few of the parents volunteered that they had problems with reading and writing. All their children were amongst the group experiencing difficulties with literacy. We met three of them, Jackie, Denise and Jane, in Chapter 6, when looking at intergenerational patterns of literacy difficulty.

I was very struck by the impression of *family* literacy difficulties in their situations, rather than problems that related to just the adult or the child on their own.

Highlighting these generational patterns of family literacy helps to show the extent of change and replication in patterns of behaviour, and also gives an indication of where support might usefully be given. This is a theme I will return to in Part Three of the book.

Summary

While most parents were actively involved in teaching their children about reading, writing, environmental print, and rhymes, many of the parents lacked confidence in this role.

The parents tended to be keen to help their children with literacy, in many ways they were able to, and in most cases they were reasonably clear about why they wished to do so.

For the majority of parents, information about literacy came from informal channels of communication, through children, family and friends, through printed matter and the media.

Half the parents remembered their own parents helping them with literacy, but many could not remember such involvement, and suggested that very large families and parents' work had made this difficult. A small number of parents had problems with reading and writing themselves, and their children were amongst the group having difficulties with literacy.

Findings from the Elmswood study suggest that most of the ways in which parents interact with their children on literacy are intuitive and come from well-embedded child-rearing practices within homes and social networks. Schools had made an impact, and some information about new methods of literacy teaching had made its way into children's homes, but this was by no means uniform, nor was information always fully understood.

We turn now to Part Three of the book, where practical implications of the findings in the Elmswood study are explored, including how to increase information and support for all parents in relation to literacy.

Part Three: Implications for Early Childhood Educators

9

Highlighting Favourite Books

The Elmswood study points to the impact of children having favourite books when they were aged three (see Appendix 3). This chapter is concerned with considering what having favourite books actually means and what implications having favourite books has in practice for those working with young children and their families.

The role of favourite books in literacy development

As Nicholas Tucker reminds us, any book or piece of writing that is meaningful for a particular child at a particular time will enrich them and become a part of their journey towards becoming more literate. In his words, we need to

> remember that less meritorious forms of writing can always have good effects should they happen to respond to their readers' particular needs at the time.
>
> (Tucker, 1993, p. 116)

Elaine Moss (1977) illustrates this with a story of her adopted daughter's affection for a cheaply produced and, in her eyes, expendable book, which contrasted with the 'great classic picture books' that she thought were much more suitable. What she came to realise was that the story's content about a little kitten that was taken in and cared for had a deep significance for her daughter who, in turn, had been taken in and looked after by her new family. She concludes that the book, although 'artistically worthless . . . hack-written and poorly illustrated', was very important for her child because its emotional content was right. It is worth bearing this story in mind before jumping to dismiss texts which do not readily conform to our ideas of what suitable reading material looks like.

On the other hand, I think it is our task as early childhood educators to give children the widest opportunities to choose from texts that have been thoughtfully produced, to extend children's reading repertoires and give them the best chance of finding reading enriching and stimulating. There are many children who have access to these experiences through a choice of reading material at home. But some other children do not have these opportunities, and it is for these children in particular that we need to ensure we provide the very best we can, and have methods of exploring with parents ways that a variety of texts may be used by children at home.

What does it mean to have favourite books at home?

In the Elmswood study having a favourite book by the age of three was an indication of later literacy achievement (see Appendix 3). This turned out to be related to a number of important literacy practices in the children's homes. So in this way, having favourite books was in fact a shorthand expression for a complex combination of early literacy experiences, which incorporated the children's access to literacy materials, their interactions with their parents, and the children's own inclinations through making choices of reading material. These relationships are shown diagrammatically in Figure 9.

The parents' interactions with the children, and the resources and opportunities they provided, were crucial. We see that the children's later achievements in literacy were influenced by such factors as whether the child had had favourite books before nursery, whether they were read to by their parents from story books, whether parents pointed out environmental print to their child, and if so, from what age, how many nursery rhymes the child knew, how often parents read to their children, the age when they first started reading to their child, whether books were read right through to them, how many books the children actually owned and if they borrowed books from the library. In this way, the notion of

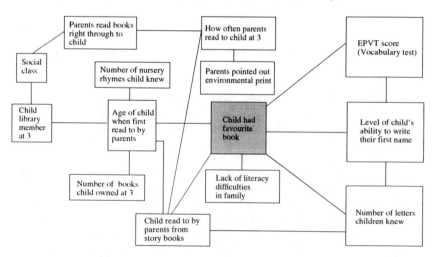

Figure 9 Relationship between having a favourite book and other factors

'favourite books' is, as I have suggested, a composite measure, a convenient and comprehensible shorthand, for a complex set of literacy practices which can encourage children's literacy development.

Having access to books that are really liked when learning to read provides children with a powerful incentive, and inbuilt gratification, for becoming a reader. Many of the parents in the Elmswood study explained that their children liked to revisit favourite books, and often were 'word perfect' on the text of these before they could read the same words out of context. For young children, re-readings of a known book can be particularly fruitful. Children come to memorise text and story, later being able to read the book for themselves, recreating the text while following the print and pictures on the correct pages. This repeating of favourite books can give children increasing experience with the language of written texts by showing how, while they always have the same words, they can mean something different each time they are read, and can be enriched by repeated rereadings. Having this familiarity with books, as observed by, and also often shared with parents, is an important part of the process of becoming a reader.

As we have discovered in the Elmswood study, many of the books with which the children were most familiar in their early years at home were actually different from the types of books they were to meet in nursery and school. Some of the books children read at home have been described in Chapter 6. What this difference in the settings of home and school implies is that those people who work with young children need to be aware of the children's early reading experiences at home, including information about the books which the children know best, and their favourite books. Some teachers now recognise the importance of helping children identify lessons from texts they know through talking with them about what they have already come to understand, instead of starting totally afresh in school. This helps the transition from home to school literacy for the less confident and less experienced children, and gives teachers deeper insights into the literacy competencies with which children come to school.

School reading books: a question of choice

Many children practise their reading in school, and at home from school books, from graded reading scheme books. These schemes provide a structured system through which children can gradually learn more complex reading strategies, including recognising a wider vocabulary, dealing with smaller print and greater length of text, dealing with increasingly complex sentence structure, and a movement towards reliance on written text and the lessening of picture and other contextual clues. All this can be very helpful to the beginning reader, but I would argue that for the older struggling reader, reading exclusively from a reading scheme reduces the chances of children learning what it is to have favourite books, which we have seen can be so important for literacy development. In the Elmswood study, for instance, by the end of the infants school only four of the forty-two children had a reading book that was not from a reading scheme. Of course this was not the only reading they did in school. However, we must bear in mind the powerful message given to children and parents by the books selected especially to help with learning to read and practise their reading. A 'reading book' implies this is what reading is about, and for some children, particularly weaker readers, this becomes the staple diet of their reading experience in school. Some of the older reading scheme books still widely used in schools have restricted and sometimes stilted language, and often lack narrative tension and dynamic interchange between pictures and text. Many newer reading scheme books are considerably more imaginative, but these are not always found in classrooms, because of lack of money. There is no doubt that controlled vocabulary can help beginner readers and children who have difficulties with reading gain confidence and limit the amount they need to learn at once. But the reading diet of struggling readers should not be confined to such books. Remember Joanne who was mentioned in Chapter 6, the unconfident reader who when asked what her favourite book was, picked the reading scheme book *Roger Red-hat*, which had a restricted storyline and limited vocabulary. While this text might possibly have been appropriate for a beginner reader at five, by the age of seven, this sort of reading material is not designed to extend children's experience of books in general, nor their experience of the world. Joanne's choice must surely have been because of limited access to other types of books from which to make a selection (as well as being probably one she felt she could manage by herself). As Henrietta Dombey (1987) points out, through access to books written for children as books in their own right, rather than just to teach reading, children can learn 'how to love books, how to choose books . . . what it is to have a favourite author', and that the consequences of not having these experiences can be serious for literacy development:

> To postpone these lessons until the reading scheme has been traversed to the end . . . is to run the very grave risk of communicating the idea that reading is something you do for someone else, or even of putting children off reading forever.
>
> (Dombey, 1987, p. 18)

While some children gain these experiences out of school, as we have seen in the Elmswood study, many children do not have access at home to these sorts of books. Most of the 'reading books' which children in the Elmswood study used at school were from reading schemes, even though other sorts of book were available. In fact, three of the four children in the Elmswood study who were using 'reading books' that were not part of a reading scheme at school, were those children who had access to similar books at home. I suggest that this had something to do with access to other types of books and therefore familiarity with them. We all tend to choose from what we know best and what is most familiar. It could have been their familiarity with such books outside school which gave these children the confidence to choose to read them in school. It is engagement with a range of texts which allows children to develop their own tastes and interests for what type of reading matter they like best, and by learning to select favourites from a number of different books, move towards becoming confident and competent readers.

For these reasons it seems important that teachers are aware not only of children's growing reading improvements, but also that they

- consciously note the range of books from which children read;
- give opportunities to learn lessons about choosing from a range of different books;
- encourage ways of expressing and developing their preferences;
- have children's choices, from both school and home, recognised and acknowledged.

Schools and governors and more widely the government must find ways of equipping teachers with the resources they need in order to foster developing readers' progress.

Books we offer children

Good books have no hallmark – and if they had one, children would probably disregard it.

(Watson, 1992, p. 1)

Adult selection is no guarantee of child pleasure, satisfaction or interest. As I have suggested earlier, children have their own special reasons for responding to books. But the wider the selection of books available, the more possibilities children have of making informed choices. Adults, who often have a wider experience of books, can help children make such choices, and show them other lessons about the pleasure and interest we can gain from looking at and reading books.

Never before has so much been published for children and it is worthwhile for adults to consider the books they make available to the children they know, whether as teachers, parents or in another capacity. I talked about the important lessons that children can learn from stories in Chapter 1, and clearly narrative is a very important form for children. As adults selecting books for children and helping children in their choice of texts, we have a number of important issues to consider. These include how well the story is told, how powerful or poetic is the language, how appealing are the illustrations and how well they work in conjunction with the written text, whether the characters come alive and if the message of the story is likely to have meaning for the young reader. This may be primarily to entertain, to give children the opportunity to explore new or difficult situations, to engage the children's emotions, for instance by comforting or frightening them, or to show children the experience of others, and different people's points of view . . . and many other possibilities besides.

While stories are a powerful form for young children, it is equally important to remember that there are non-fiction texts which have wide appeal, and from which children also learn important lessons about accessing information for themselves, and beginning to understand aspects of the world and their relationship to it. From these books, children can learn how to use texts in a non-linear way, with use, for instance, of contents pages and indexes, learning to take the meaning they want from within a larger book, and in their use of books, being active learners negotiating their own meanings.

It is helpful if adults presenting books to children select them thoughtfully, paying attention to the criteria suggested above, as well as having regard for the appropriateness of style and size of the print, the amount of print on a page, and to other issues that may be of concern, such as avoiding racism and sexism.

Adults have a significant role in encouraging children to become readers, and by providing appropriate resources, of course not forgetting the importance of sharing books together with the children, they can help them explore meanings and give them strategies for dealing with what the words actually say.

Increasing access to books

Poor readers often have a lack of experience in reading from a range of books. I think their predicament is like the old saying of not being able to see the wood for the trees. The argument sometimes is that children have difficulties with reading, therefore they need simplified texts which do not challenge them, or which put them off by being too unlike what they have encountered before. Effort is concentrated on attending only to the details of individual simple texts (the trees) rather than also allowing children to acquire an overview of the whole process by gaining an understanding of how a range of texts work (the wood). However, I rather think it is often the other way around. Because the children are struggling, and we have seen that children with literacy difficulties are less likely than other children to have much experience of a range of books at home, they are confined to a very limited range of texts that do not provide a satisfactory explanation to the children of what reading is about, nor do they offer a satisfying narrative or non-fiction account from which children can derive gratification. The task becomes to get to the end of the book, rather than to read 'for a particular purpose'. As proficient readers we do not on the whole read as an end in itself, but rather to amuse or inform ourselves.

This purpose is often not apparent to weaker readers. It is through experience of books, and especially of learning what it is to choose and engage with their favourite books, that children may come to understand about the central purpose of reading. We need to give all children wider opportunities and experience, then the children can start to see the wood rather than the trees, the process rather than some of its components.

If we are to encourage children to have favourite books, and allow the literacy practices which encourage this to flourish (at home and at school), we need to ensure that children have good access to books. There are many ways of increasing access to books; through bookclubs, both in school and by mail order to the parents' homes, through libraries, through special activities which have books as their focus, and through displaying and disseminating information about books. All or each of these may be worth considering for your own situation. In the next section I look more specifically at the practicalities of extending the range of books available to children.

Bookclubs

There are two main ways in which schools can run their own children's bookclubs. One method is for the school to have a selection of books available for parents and children to look at and browse through before they buy their own copies. This has the advantage of having opportunities for 'hands-on' browsing and selecting by children and parents. It does have storage and staffing implications which need to be considered. However, it does not have to be time-consuming or onerous, and can indeed be a good point of contact between school staff and parents, and one where literacy issues can be explored. Often these schemes also have a system whereby children can save up for books by buying savings stamps. An example of this would be the Wise Owl Bookshops, run by:

Books for Students Ltd
Bird Road
Heathcote
Warwick
CV34 6TB
Tel: (01926) 314366

The second method involves sending regular newsletters published by a commercial bookclub home with the individual children. These advertise a selection of books, which children pay for in advance. The books are then ordered by the school, and are distributed from there. An example of such a scheme is Red House, which can be contacted at:

The Red House
School Book Club
Cotswold Business Park
Witney
OX8 5YF
Tel: (01993) 708225

There are of course also numerous bookclubs that will send children's books through the post, often at discounted prices. Choice is usually made from a picture, and possibly a short caption. These are widely advertised in newspapers and magazines, or catalogues and fliers may be sent directly to people's homes. Parents may wish to use these bookclubs as a way of extending their children's book collection, or their own. Seeing copies of the actual books in a school or library can sometimes help with selection.

Other books by post

Madeleine Lindley Ltd is a specialist bookcentre which provides children's books and also books about literacy mail order for teachers and others who may be interested, and which also acts as a mobile bookshop for conferences and other events. Visitors can visit the bookcentre to browse and buy from their extensive selection of books. Much thought and effort is placed on selecting books and advising people of appropriate up-to-date books. The contact address and phone number is:

Madeleine Lindley Ltd
BookCentre
79 and 90 Acorn Centre
Barry Street
Oldham
OL1 3NE
Tel: (0161) 627 5820/(0161) 620 3001

Letterbox Library is a mail order company which specialises in non-sexist and multi-cultural books for children. They publish quarterly catalogues and newsletters, and also have around a dozen local contacts who can arrange displays of books at schools and centres. The address and phone number is:

Letterbox Library
2D Leroy House
436 Essex Road
London
N1 3QP
Tel: (0171) 226 1633

Libraries

Libraries are an extremely important source of access to a wide range of books, which until recently have been generally available, and which allowed children and their families to have experience with different types of books from others they may have local access to, for instance, those available in supermarkets and newsagents. In recent years, libraries have been faced with cuts in funding, opening hours, and closures of local branch libraries. All this threatens the availability of books to ordinary families in their communities.

As well as public libraries which often have separate children's sections and a children's librarian with specialist knowledge about children's books, with whom you might be able to liaise, there are often a range of community organisations which might well incorporate loaning children's books – or might be encouraged to do so! These might include:

- local schools
- individual classes within school
- nursery units, classes, schools or day nurseries
- family centres
- parent and toddler groups
- playgroups

Each community organisation needs to establish a source of books, and devise a system for sending books home, and a method of recording books going home. It is interesting to see which books are most often borrowed, and how widely the service is being used.

Special activities that have books as their focus

There are a number of local activities that can draw attention to books. These could include:

- bookfairs
- sales of books – new and second-hand
- exchange of books
- book diaries
- book reviews
- 'book of the week' – displays in schools, centres and shops
- book making
- organising visits to libraries in small groups
- organising visits to bookshops in small groups

Displaying and disseminating information about books

There are a number of ways in which parents can be given information about books. These could include posters, for instance showing favourite books, children's authors, new publications, photos of children reading, children's comments and parents' comments.

You might like to design your own material, or use it in conjunction with items that have been produced elsewhere. The Reading and Language Information Centre, for instance, has a number of pamphlets aimed at parents which you might find useful. They include:

- *Books to share at home with children aged 0–3 years, 3–5 years and 5–7 years*
- *Preparing your child for reading. Advice for parents of 2–5 year olds*
- *How to help your child with reading. Advice for parents of children 4–7 years*
- *How to help your child with writing. Advice for parents of children 3–7 years*

The address and phone number of the Centre is:

The Reading and Language Information Centre
University of Reading
Bulmershe Court
Earley
Reading
RG6 1HY
Tel: (01734) 318820

Another way of reaching people is by distributing leaflets and newsletters; for example, with details of where to pick up books in town – bookshops and other places such as W. H. Smith, Early Learning Centre, Bargain Bookshops, or information including book reviews and comments about favourite books.

Increasing access to books in your own context

It is worth bearing in mind the needs of the particular community in which you work. It could be instructive, for instance, to find out what is available in local shops. It may be worth surveying what is already available, and the needs and interests of children and parents in your area. In this way you can build up a picture of what already exists, and see where the gaps are, if you are thinking of establishing a new form of book provision. You may also think about people working in other organisations with whom it would be appropriate for you to work. This might include librarians, health visitors, under-fives workers, youth workers, those working in playgroups, parent and toddler groups, creches, and maybe a community group particular to your own situation. Then the task is to obtain the books you need, or give information to others to get books for themselves, and decide how your scheme will operate. Once you are involved in any form of increasing access to books, it is always valuable to do some sort of evaluation, to see how things are going, and what you might do next.

In summary, to increase access to books you could:

- establish local need through a survey;
- explore partnership possibilities;
- obtain the books or information you need;
- establish a system;
- evaluate your scheme;
- use this to plan what you do next.

We must bear in mind in particular the children who do not yet have favourite books, and find ways of encouraging them and their parents to engage with books so the children can gain more experience, and from that the satisfactions and literacy lessons that come from being a real 'reader'. In devising ways to increase access to books, we need to try in particular to reach everybody, and not just a small minority who may already be well-resourced.

In this chapter we have looked specifically at the issue of children having favourite books. This may vary in the different contexts of home and school, and we have already in previous chapters looked at the way the literacies of home and school may differ. In the next chapter we look more closely at how we can build connections between the literacy contexts of home and school, and how we can try to ensure communication between schools and *all* parents, for the benefit of the children's literacy learning.

10

Extending Home–School Relations

In this chapter we review the findings of the Elmswood study which point to the importance of home–school relations for children's literacy development. But the main thrust of the chapter is practical – what might extended home–school relations look like? To help those working in a school setting, I have devised a Matrix which allows you to look at your current practice on work with parents concerning literacy, and which gives clear guidelines for extending your practice, should you choose to do so.

What have home–school relations to offer literacy learning?

Work with parents is a growing area of interest and concern in schools. But many teachers have not been led to expect that work with parents would be required (Nutbrown, Hannon and Weinberger, 1991), as well as delivering a crowded curriculum to increasing numbers of children. Yet as we have already seen, children's literacy performance can be positively affected by the contribution parents make. Parents' knowledge about literacy teaching in school, and their interactions with teachers, can help children's literacy learning. The Elmswood study has confirmed findings from other research that contact between teachers and parents on literacy can significantly affect children's reading and has shown that this is true for writing as well. What the study has also done is to replicate findings from other research which showed that teachers tended to work more with the parents who already knew most about school literacy practices (Toomey, 1989).

While some teachers may still be unclear about whether parents are involved and interested in their children's literacy, the Elmswood study highlights the interest most parents show in helping their child with literacy (see also Newson and Newson, 1977, Hall *et al.*, 1989, Hannon and James, 1990).

Given the weight of this evidence, it would appear that work on extending home–school relations will directly benefit children in their literacy learning.

What this means for practice

The Elmswood study shows that literacy learning which takes place in families needs to be made more visible to teachers, so that it can be built on, and enhanced, at school. Children's literacy development would be helped if teachers talked more with parents about literacy occurring as a part of everyday family activities at home; about the parents' role in providing resources and opportunities; about parents acting as a model for literacy, and interacting with their child on literacy. Teachers could provide more information to *all* parents about the literacy teaching in school. It is particularly important to include the less confident parents of children with relatively low competence in literacy. If teachers encourage reading books to go home, it would be helpful if teachers ensured *all* children were reminded that they could take their book, and a system of encouragement devised. It would be useful if teachers could check that parents knew about their role in this, and that they were happy about how often the books went home. Many of the parents I spoke to in the Elmswood study would have liked their child to bring a book home more frequently.

For early years teachers, it would help to find out more about the home experiences of children who did not choose books for themselves in a nursery setting. It would also be useful to discover how many rhymes the children knew already, and to encourage saying rhymes at home, particularly for those children whose experience here was limited. Teachers could also find out about children's story book experience at home, and whether they had access to a library, and add encouragement. Teachers of young children could ask parents about children's favourite books. For those without favourites, teachers could suggest the family borrow books, show parents the range of books available for young children (as discussed in Chapter 9) and explain how important it is for children to have the opportunity and encouragement to choose a favourite book for later literacy development. Teachers could talk with parents about the children's writing at home, and what experiences they had of mark making. It would be helpful to share information about ordinary day-to-day activities which might well include literacy, highlighting for parents what they were already doing and offering support and encouragement.

What have we got to gain?

There is a lot to be gained on both sides by parents and teachers communicating effectively with one another. Here is a summary of some of the main relative strengths of the school and the home as contexts for children's literacy learning.

Teachers' expertise	Parents' expertise
• Detailed knowledge about children at a particular age	• Detailed knowledge about their own particular child
• Knowledge of ways of helping children with particular literacy problems	• Knowledge of how literacy is used in their particular home and community
• Knowledge of the curriculum, and what has previously been taught in school	• Knowledge of their own child's personal history
• Relationship with children during school hours and activities, including literacy practices	• Relationship with their child out of school hours including literacy practices
• Showing children about what literacy means in a school setting	• Showing children about what literacy means in a home setting

If a child is to benefit most fully from the literacy learning potentially available to them, both school and home/community uses of literacy need to be taken into account. This is in terms of what is read and written about, and how they are used.

What sort of communication?

As well as considering the need for increased communication, it is also worth asking what sort of exchange and communication is most effective. During the course of writing this book, my husband became seriously ill. I was increasingly struck with the parallels between his experiences, and a child's progress in literacy, and also the relationships between professionals and patient/learner and their family. I think we can learn from this about the style of communication that is most helpful.

These were the approaches by the professionals who were involved in dealing with my husband's illness that really helped:

• recognising the centrality of family in the process
• allowing the family to remain in control
• acknowledging that we were active in the process
• taking us seriously
• giving encouragement
• treating us without condescension
• giving us clear information
• giving us responsibility
• allowing us ownership of what was going on

- showing an interest, even when views may have differed
- listening with open-mindedness
- showing a willingness to share the process of what was going on
- not hiding behind technical jargon

These were ways of reacting both to my husband, as the patient, and also to me and the family as his supporters and carers. Far from us being peripheral to the healing/learning process, I think we were central, and we had an important part to play in mediating the institutional (hospital and doctor) experience. I think that all these elements of how professionals share and interact with interested parties are relevant to teachers and parents.

The Home–School Literacy Evaluation Matrix

The Matrix in Figure 10 is a diagnostic tool which can be used to establish a profile for your school's approach to parental involvement in literacy. It has been adapted from a tried and tested tool used in energy management (BRECSU, 1993). Although this may seem a very different area, many of the ideas are directly applicable here. I am grateful to colleagues who have used this Matrix with teachers in schools for their helpful feedback during the pilot phase of designing the instrument.

The profile can be used to review the current state of parental involvement in literacy in your school, and to identify which areas you wish to develop. It is a tool for identifying current strengths and weaknesses in terms of the school's approach to parental involvement in literacy. As we have seen a school initiative on parental involvement in literacy is of benefit to the children.

Each column of the matrix deals with one of six key issues:

- School policy on parents and literacy
- Record-keeping and assessment of literacy including parents
- Written documentation for parents on literacy and its dissemination
- Formal contact with parents concerning literacy
- Informal contact with parents concerning literacy
- Knowledge of children's home literacy

The ascending rows, from 1 to 5, represent increasingly developed responses to these issues. The aim for schools who wish to increase their profile on parental involvement in literacy would be to move up through these levels, and also, if this were relevant to your individual circumstances, see if a balance across the columns would be appropriate, so complementing policy with practice, and formal with informal methods of communication (see Figure 11).

The Home–School Literacy Evaluation Matrix

Level	School policy on parents & literacy including children reading school books at home, parents helping in school	Record keeping and assessment of literacy including parents	Written documentation for parents on literacy and its dissemination	Formal contact with parents concerning literacy	Informal contact with parents concerning literacy	Knowledge of children's home literacy
5	A policy shared by all staff, frequently reviewed that works in practice	Record keeping and assessment which involves parents in discussion and recording, under review, and up-to-date	Well-presented and jargon-free information for parents, which is up-to-date. Given to all parents, in all appropriate languages	Combination of parent-teacher consultations and sessions to explain teaching of literacy to parents, well-attended and backed up for non-attenders by home visits or letters or phone calls	Frequent contact with all parents concerning literacy	Detailed knowledge about home literacy for all children
4	An unwritten set of guidelines	Record keeping and assessment which involves parents in either recording or discussion	Written documentation available, but requires updating	Formal contact with most parents	Frequent informal contact with most parents	Detailed knowledge about home literacy for most children (which ones)
3	Formal policy, but not used in practice	Record keeping and assessment which involves some parents	Written documentation available, but not well presented	Formal contact with some parents	Infrequent informal contact with parents	A little knowledge about home literacy for most children
2	Different teachers have different policies, with varying degrees of success	Record keeping and assessment which involves few parents	Written documentation available, but no system for documents to reach all parents	Formal contact with few parents and no alternative back-up of home visits or letters or phone calls	Informal contact with few parents	Knowledge about home literacy for a few children (which ones)
1	No explicit policy	No involvement of parents in record keeping or assessment	No written documentation for parents	Formal contact with parents on literacy at minimal level	No informal contact with parents	No knowledge about home literacy for any children

© Jo Weinberger, 1996

Figure 10   The Home–School Literacy Evaluation Matrix

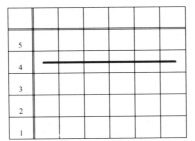

Balanced matrix

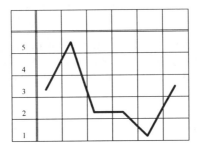

Unbalanced matrix

Figure 11   Examples of a balanced and unbalanced Matrix

Ways of using the Home–School Literacy Evaluation Matrix to promote change in school

This is an exercise in which individual teachers work on their own responses initially, and then pool their responses to create a whole school profile and action plan.

For each teacher in school and headteacher individually

This can be done on your own, or you may decide to do it individually at the start of a staff meeting or INSET day at which you discuss the school's approach to parental involvement in literacy.

1. Make a photocopy of the matrix. Consider each column, one at a time. Then mark the place in each column which best describes where you think you are currently located. Place your mark in the appropriate cell, or between cells if that seems more accurate. For legibility it can be helpful to do this with a highlighter pen.
2. Join up your marks across the columns to produce a graph line. This is the profile of your approach to parental involvement in literacy. It will

give an overall indication of how balanced your approach is in terms of policy and practice, formality and informality.

Don't worry if the profile is uneven. This is what happens for most teachers and most schools. The peaks indicate where current effort is most developed; the troughs areas where policy or practice is least advanced.

For teachers and headteacher together

3. When each teacher, and headteacher, has completed an individual copy of the Matrix, these can be compared at a time which you set aside for staff discussion. Where the profiles disagree, discuss your assessments to see if you can reach a shared position. If you can agree a shared profile, draw it on a new photocopy of the Matrix.

If you can't agree, draw the different profiles on a new photocopy of the Matrix, and label them as your separate views. This process gives all teachers a chance to have their perspective viewed, discussed and recorded.

4. The next step is to agree on a way to move forward. Talk together about which columns contain issues that are most important in your school setting.

It will not always be the columns where you score lowest which warrant immediate attention. There may be some issues where there do not seem to be obvious opportunities for improvement at present, and you may be better off investing your limited time and attention elsewhere.

5. Date your collated profiles. Then, after discussion, formulate and record an action plan for the next twelve months, showing how the school intends to improve its profile on parental involvement in literacy. It should be clear who is responsible for any of the actions listed. Set a date for reviewing progress, when changes to the profiles can be recorded, and further action decided.

Any change in your school's approach to parental involvement in literacy needs to be consciously managed, and you need to plan:

- what you are trying to achieve;
- how you intend to achieve it;
- whose help and assistance you will need along the way;
- whose resistance you will have to overcome to be successful;
- intermediate milestones so you can tell how much you are achieving.

Identifying your own strengths and weaknesses

There is no single action plan for improvement which will suit all schools. You need to tailor one to your own specific requirements. Even similar schools may find themselves in quite different situations, depending on what they are already doing in terms of parental involvement in literacy, and how successful they have been to date.

The end point of using this Matrix, and of extending home–school relations generally, is for early childhood educators to work more closely with parents for the benefit of children's literacy learning.

In this book we have looked mainly at the development of children's literacy from a parents' perspective. Early childhood educators can now add this perspective to their own, to create a more comprehensive view of the different worlds of literacy that children inhabit, and in so doing, enhance the potential of all children to make sense of what it is to be literate.

An increased exchange of information about home literacy and about school literacy will help bring the positive and diverse aspects of home literacy to the attention of those working in schools, and clarify aspects of school literacy which still mystify parents. The beneficiaries of the process of increased mutual understanding and on-going dialogue may be the adults, but, most importantly, the main beneficiaries are all the children learning to be literate in our complex modern world.

Appendix 1

Framework for Looking at the Influence of Parents on their Children's Literacy Development

This framework provides the underlying structure for the discussion of findings from the Elmswood Study.

The role of parents in the context of their children's literacy learning includes: an awareness of their role and of literacy development; how they resourced literacy in the home; and the way they behaved as 'teachers' and how they interacted with their children on literacy practices and events. To help clarify this I devised a framework for looking at the role of parents in their children's literacy development. (The thinking behind the framework was informed by work with Peter Hannon, 1990.) This provided a tool for examining the parents' contribution, to show

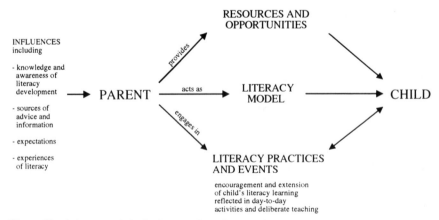

Figure 12 A framework for looking at the influence of parents on their children's literacy development

some of the influences on the parents, and the ways in which the parents influenced the child. This framework appears in Figure 12.

The framework shows some of the influences that may affect parents' behaviour, including sources of advice and information, contact they may have with their child's school, their experience and expectations, and their knowledge and awareness of literacy development.

To varying extents, parents provide resources and opportunities for literacy for their children (for instance, supplying books, going on a shopping expedition involving some reading and writing). They may also act as a literacy model (for example, by reading a newspaper, or writing a shopping list). They may also interact with their child on literacy practices and events, on an informal basis, without necessarily consciously thinking about the literacy teaching involved, or through deliberate teaching. The two-way arrow in the Figure indicates that these activities are interactive with the child. (Resourcing and modelling may also be interactive, but they are not inherently so.)

Appendix 2

Background to the Elmswood Study

Context of the Elmswood Study

The Elmswood study looked at children's literacy practices and achievements at different times; in most detail when the children were aged three and aged seven, but also when they were aged five.

All the children in the Elmswood study had attended the same nursery. This and the school to which it was attached were situated on the edge of a council housing estate. Because many of the houses had several bedrooms, and their own gardens, a number of the families had been re-housed from the inner city, and there were in general large numbers of families with young children housed on the estate. There was also a high rise block in which a number of families with children lived. In addition, there was a traditional village, which had older private housing, a mixture of terraces, flats and one or two larger properties, and also a growing number of private housing estates nearby. Because of the mixed nature of the housing, this meant that the children coming to nursery were from a wide variety of social backgrounds, and their parents had differing educational experiences.

Families operate within complex social networks, and even very young children interact with many different people. To gain some insight into the key people in the children's lives, I asked parents about other significant people involved in looking after the children. Only one of the children lived in an extended family at the start of the study (with grandparents). One other child lived with her grandparents until the age of two, and many lived near their relatives. For nearly half the children, grandparents played a significant role in their daily lives, looking after them regularly, and for over a quarter of the children, aunts and uncles sometimes looked after them. Close neighbours and people from the local church were also often important as care-givers, and some of the children were looked after outside the 'extended' family circle, by childminders or 'babysitters'.

There were few families in the area from ethnic minority groups. In the study itself, all the families were white and spoke English as a first language, apart from one where English was a second language. Many of the most local children who attended the nursery and lived in the immediate vicinity continued through the infants school, although some children who lived further afield went to a number of other primary schools.

Initially there were sixty children in the study, twenty-six girls and thirty-four boys. By the time the children reached the end of the infants school, at age seven or thereabouts, there were forty-two children in the study. This means that in Chapter 5, where I consider children's literacy at home at three, I am describing the experiences of all sixty children and parents, but in subsequent chapters, I record the experiences of forty-two children and their parents.

The word 'parents' is used throughout, but this needs some clarification. It is customary to refer to parents even when, as in this case, one is dealing primarily with mothers. In the Elmswood study, I talked with each child's mother, although in a few cases I talked with their father as well. This happened because I had contact with the families during the daytime, and this was when the majority of the mothers had sole responsibility for childcare. What these mothers (and occasionally fathers) were doing was providing the 'parent' as opposed to the 'school' perspective on children's literacy learning.

Appendix 3

Measures of Literacy: Home Experiences and School Literacy

Because the Elmswood study was a longitudinal one, it was possible to explore whether any of the children's early literacy experiences at home before nursery, and at school entry, had a relationship with the children's later literacy development. This appendix supplies quantitative rather than qualitative information and makes use of statistics. The messages, however, about the importance and relevance of what happens at home, in terms of children's literacy development, remain the same as those in the rest of the book.

Information about the children's literacy in the Elmswood study was collected when they were aged three, five and seven. When the children were aged three, parents were interviewed at home, to give details of the children's family background, and issues relating to literacy resources and practices at home. At age five, assessments were carried out of children's vocabulary, writing, letter knowledge, their access to stories at home and their use of books in the nursery. At age seven, children were interviewed, as were the parents for a second time, to provide updated information about families, and literacy in the home.

The five measures of children's literacy at seven were children's standardised reading test scores (Young's Group Reading Test, 1989); a writing score; the level of their reading book used in class, using a system devised by Moon (1980), levels reached on Standard Assessment Tasks for English (School Examinations and Assessment Council, 1991, 1992); and whether the children were judged to be having literacy difficulties. Children whose scores fell within the bottom third on two or more measures of literacy at this stage were judged to be having literacy difficulties. The children identified in this way were also those who, according to their teachers' judgements, were experiencing problems with literacy. (More details of the assessments and measurement are in Weinberger, 1993.)

Home experiences at three and reading book level

Statistical techniques were used to find out whether any of the literacy practices at home early on suggest a relationship with children's reading level later. A number of different methods were used, including comparison of group means, correlations and chi squared tests. Whether children had favourite books by age three emerged as a significant factor. Having favourite books or not reflects several aspects of early book experience, including children's access to materials, their interactions with parents, and their own inclinations through making choices. Using a comparison of group means, it emerged that the 15 per cent of children who were reported as not having favourite books by age three had a mean reading book level of 4.9, compared to 7.8 for the others (F (1,40) = 9.6, p < .01).

As in other studies, employment and social class showed significant associations here with later reading book level. Thirteen of the mothers were employed outside the home when the children were aged three, mostly on a part-time, casual basis. Their children's mean reading book level was 8.7 compared with a mean level of 6.6 for the children whose mothers had not been employed (F (1,40) = 6.5, p < .01). In terms of class, children from middle class homes had a mean reading book level of 8.5, while children from working class homes had a mean level of 6.5 (F (1,40) = 6.3, p < .05).

Sensitivity to rhyme has been shown in other studies to be connected with later literacy achievement. In the Elmswood study, the children's reported knowledge of nursery rhymes was used as a measure of rhyme sensitivity. Parents of fifteen children said their children knew more than a dozen nursery rhymes before going to nursery. Their children later had a mean reading book level of 8.5. The remaining children knew fewer rhymes and had a mean reading level of 6.5 (F (1,40) = 3.9, p < .05). For very young children, much of their knowledge of nursery rhymes was likely to come from experiences at home, with parents repeating and singing familiar rhymes with them.

Another factor which showed a relationship with later level of reading book was whether the children were library members at age three. It was of course the children's parents who would have chosen whether to enrol them in the library. Only eleven children were library members at three. Their later reading book level was 8.7, compared with a level of 6.7 for the other children (F (1,40) = 3.9, p < .05). In this way access to reading material at a young age suggests a relationship with progress in learning to read.

In addition, I asked parents what sorts of material they read with their children at age three. Six children were not read to from story books. These particular children later had a lower mean level of reading book than the other children (a level of 5.3 compared with 7.6, F (1,40) = 3.9, p < .05).

Taken together these findings show that the parents' interactions with books with their children had a positive influence on the later literacy development.

School entry literacy and reading book level

Several assessments of children's literacy achievements at school entry turned out to be related significantly to their reading book level at age seven. The highest correlation was for the children's scores on vocabulary tests, namely for the WPPSI Vocabulary Subtest (Wechsler, 1967), $r = 0.55$, $p < .001$, and for the English Picture Vocabulary Test (EPVT, Brimer and Dunn, 1963), $r = 0.53$, $p < .001$. What also turned out to be highly significant was how competently the children were able to write their first name, $r = 0.53$, $p < .001$. The children's ability to write their name at this stage would have been influenced by their own inclinations and abilities, but also by the help and guidance of supportive adults. Also highly significant was the relationship between whether the child knew some letters or not and the level of reading book at age seven, $r = 0.51$, $p < .001$. The children's ability to copy a phrase was significantly related to later reading book level. Those that could do so later had a mean reading level of 8.0 compared with a mean level of 6.3 (F $(1,39) = 5.0$, $p < .05$). This assessment was one that gave an indication of the children's familiarity with reproducing standard letter shapes. This finding indicates the interrelatedness of reading and writing. The parents were asked how often children listened to stories at home. Fifteen children listened to stories at home at least once a day, and they had a higher mean reading book level (8.1) than those for whom this was more infrequent (6.5, F $(1,39) = 4.4$, p $< .05$). Children's familiarity and enjoyment of books at home probably made the children more likely to choose to look at books on their own when they came to nursery. Twenty-nine of the forty-two children did so of their own initiative, and this was significantly associated with the level of reading book at age seven (mean reading levels of 8.0 and 5.5, F $(1,40) = 9.4$, $p < .01$).

What these findings indicate is that the knowledge children brought with them from home and nursery at school entry shows a significant relationship with how well they were reading later on at school. The more they already knew about literacy at five, the more likely they were to be reading well at seven.

Home experiences at age seven and reading book level

There were a number of home experiences at age seven related to the children's reading book level. Fourteen of the children had access to a computer at home at this stage, and many of their parents gave examples of how this helped the children's literacy. They had a mean reading book level of 8.1 compared with a mean level of 5.5 for the other children (F $(1,40) = 11.4$, $p < .01$). It is not, however, clear from this study whether it was the interaction with the computer as such that was important, or whether this referred to some underlying feature of the home, for instance the level of resourcing or general interest in education.

The parents' own perceptions of their role with regard to literacy and school were significant in relation to children's level of reading book. Only twelve of the forty-two parents felt they knew how reading was taught in school. Their children had a mean reading book level of 8.9 compared with the mean level of the other children of 6.6 (F (1,40) = 4.4, p < .01). Similarly, only ten parents said they knew about writing in school. Their children had a mean reading book level of 8.7, while the other children had a mean level of 6.8 (F (1,40) = 4.4, p < .05). Thus, those parents who had more knowledge of school literacy practices tended to have children with a higher level of reading book at age seven. Two-thirds of the children said they were aware of seeing someone reading at home. Their mean reading book level, at 7.9, was higher than that for the other children, at 5.9 (F (1,40) = 6.5, p < .01). In this way, parents, acting as models for literacy, probably had an impact on the children's reading at school.

Taken as a whole, these findings show the considerable impact that parents and the family context make on children's literacy development, influencing the level of reading book children were likely to use in school. The picture which emerges is one where children reading well are those whose literacy was resourced at home, allowing them experience of favourite books, whose parents read stories to them, and maybe as a consequence, these children chose to look at books in nursery. The children saw their parents read at home, and the parents themselves had some idea about literacy teaching in school.

Children reading to parents and reading test scores

Young's Group Reading Test was used (Young, 1989). Many of the test findings were similar to those already mentioned for the level of child's reading book.

A finding that is worth mentioning here, as it has been explored in other research studies, is about children reading to their parents at home. Whether children read aloud at home either everyday or nearly every day, or did not do so, was significantly associated with YGRT score (r = 0.26, p < .05). This relationship has also been found in relation to standardised reading test scores in some other studies (Hewison and Tizard, 1980, Hannon, 1987). However, Tizard *et al.* (1988) did not find a relationship between how often children read aloud at home and later literacy performance, and they speculate that this may have been because other studies took place in settings where there was more support for the parents and teachers. While the Elmswood study did show some relationship, further studies into the role of parents hearing their children read at home are needed.

Children with literacy difficulties

In educational terms, it is helpful to know whether there are any factors which are likely to be associated with literacy problems at age seven. In the Elmswood study, fourteen children were identified (see p. 148) as having literacy problems. For children with literacy difficulties, as for the other children, a number of factors turned out to be significantly associated with their level of reading book at age seven. These included their vocabulary score (EPVT), how well they could write their name and copy a phrase, and whether they knew some letters or not. All had a significant relationship with their reading book at age seven ($p < .001$). In addition, whether the child had favourite books by age three, the number of nursery rhymes the child knew, the children's vocabulary score (WPPSI Vocabulary Subtest), and whether they chose to look at books at nursery were also significantly associated with the reading book level of children with literacy difficulties at age seven ($p < .01$). Parents of children having difficulties were less likely to know how reading was taught in school and therefore were less able to offer help with literacy problems at school.

There were also other factors. Children with literacy difficulties were less likely to read to someone frequently at home (2 (1) = 8.9, $p < .01$), and were less likely, according to their teacher, to take school reading books home (2 (1) = 5.8, $p < .01$). Thus the more problems they had, the less likely they were to read voluntarily, so making it hard to get the practice and experience they needed to improve. Their parents were also amongst those who, when I asked them questions relating to day-to-day literacy learning activities at home, were not able to provide examples (2 (1) = 5.8, $p < .01$). It may well be that this reflected a lack of parental awareness about children's literacy learning.

Resourcing of literacy was also relevant here. Children with literacy problems owned on average fewer books than other children (2 (2) = 7.1, $p < .05$), and were less likely to have access to a computer at home at age seven (2 (1) = 3.9, $p < .05$). These factors were also reflected in their teachers' judgement that these children were receiving less support for literacy from home than the other children (2 (1) = 3.6, $p < .05$). So the children with literacy difficulties had less experience, fewer resources and less support than other children. The implication is that children need greater access to literacy resources and encouragement to use them and their parents need more information and support, so that they in turn can better support the children.

All the findings I have discussed here give *quantitative* evidence to substantiate the *qualitative* findings of the Elmswood study, discussed in the earlier chapters, namely that the parents and the home have a significant part to play in young children's early literacy development. It is how parents interact with their child on literacy, and the literacy climate of the homes, that is shown in this study to have an influence on children's literacy performance in school.

References

Adams, M. J. (1990) *Beginning to Read: Thinking and Learning About Print*, Cambridge, Massachusetts, London: MIT Press.

Anbar, A. (1986) Reading acquisition of preschool children without systematic instruction, *Early Childhood Research Quarterly*, Vol. 1, no. 1, pp. 69–83.

Applebee, A. N. (1978) *The Child's Concept of Story: Two to Seventeen*, Chicago and London: University of Chicago Press.

Ashton C. and Jackson, J. (1986) 'Lies, damned lies, and statistics': or a funny thing happened in a reading project, *AEP Journal*, pp. 43–6.

Baghban, M. (1984) *Our Daughter Learns to Read and Write: a Case Study from Birth to Three*, Newark, Delaware: International Reading Association.

Barrs, M., Ellis, S., Hester, H. and Thomas, A. (1989) *Patterns of Learning: the Primary Language Record and the National Curriculum*, London: ILEA/Centre for Language in Primary Education.

Barrs, M. and Pidgeon, S. (eds.) (1993) *Reading the Difference: Gender and Reading in the Primary School*, London: Centre for Language in Primary Education.

Barton, D. (1994) *Literacy: an Introduction to the Ecology of Written Language*, Oxford: Blackwell.

Beard, R. (ed.) (1993) *Teaching Literacy: Balancing Perspectives*, Sevenoaks, Kent: Hodder & Stoughton.

Bissex, G. L. (1980) *GYNS at WRK: A Child Learns to Write and Read*, Cambridge, M.A.: Harvard University Press.

Blatchford, P. (1991) Children's writing at seven years: associations with handwriting on school entry and preschool factors, *British Journal of Educational Psychology*, Vol. 61, pp. 73–84.

Blatchford, P., Battle, S. and Mays, J. (1982) *The First Transition: Home to Preschool*, Windsor, Berks: NFER-Nelson.

Blatchford, P., Burke, J., Farquhar, C., Plewis, I. and Tizard, B. (1985) Educational achievement in the infant school: the influence of ethnic origin, gender and home on entry skills, *Educational Research*, Vol. 27, no. 1, pp. 52–60.

Bradley, L. and Bryant, P. (1983) Categorising sounds and learning to read: a causal connection, *Nature*, no. 301, pp. 419–21.

Bradley, L. and Bryant, P. (1985) *Rhyme and Reason in Reading and Spelling*, IARLD Monographs, no. 1, Ann Arbor, University of Michigan Press.

BRECSU (1993) *Reviewing Energy Management*, Watford: Building Research Establishment.

Brimer, A. and Dunn, L. (1963) *English Picture Vocabulary Test*, Windsor, Berks: NFER.

Bruner, J. S. (1975) Language as an instrument of thought, in A. Davies (ed.) *Problems of Language and Learning*, London: Heinemann.

Bruner, J. (1987) The transactional self, in J. Bruner and H. Haste (eds.) *Making Sense: the Child's Construction of the World*, London: Methuen.

Bryant, P. E., Bradley, L., Maclean, M. and Crossland, J. (1989) Nursery rhymes, phonological skills and reading, *Journal of Child Language*, Vol. 16, pp. 407–28.

Butler, D. (1979) *Cushla and Her Books*, London: Hodder & Stoughton.

Chall, J. S. (1967) *Learning to Read: the Great Debate*, New York: McGraw-Hill.

Clark, M. (1976) *Young Fluent Readers*, London: Heinemann Educational.

Crago, M. and Crago, H. (1983) *Prelude to Literacy: a Preschool Child's Encounter with Picture and Story*, Carbondale, Illinois: Southern Illinois University Press.

Davie, R., Butler, N. and Goldstein, H. (1972) *From Birth to Seven*, London: Longman.

Department of Education and Science (1967) *Children and Their Primary Schools*, Volume 1 (The Plowden Report), London: HMSO.

Department of Education and Science (1988) *Report of the Committee of Inquiry into the Teaching of English Language (Kingman Report)*, London: HMSO.

Department of Education and Science (1990) *English in the National Curriculum*, London: HMSO.

Dickinson, D. K., de Temple, J. M., Hirschler, J. A. and Smith, M. W. (1992) Book reading with preschoolers: co-construction of text at home and at school, *Early Childhood Research Quarterly*, Vol. 7, no. 3, pp. 323–46.

Dombey, H. (1987) Reading for real from the start, *English in Education*, Vol. 21, pp. 12–19.

Dombey, H. (1992) *Words and Worlds: Reading in the Early Years of School*, York: Longman NAAE and NATE.

Dowker, A. (1989) Rhymes and alliteration in poems elicited from young children, *Journal of Child Language*, Vol. 16, pp. 181–202.

Durkin, D. (1961) Children who learned to read at home, *Elementary School Journal*, Vol. 62, p. 15.

Durkin, D. (1966) *Children Who Read Early*, New York: Teachers College Press.

Ehri, L. C. (1983) A critique of five studies related to letter-name knowledge and learning to read, in L. M. Gentile, M. L. Kamil and J. S. Blandchard (eds.) *Reading Research Revisited*, Columbus, OH: Charles E. Merrill.

Epstein, J. L. (1988) How do we improve programs for parent involvement? *Educational Horizons*, Vol. 66, pp. 58–9.

Epstein, J. L. (1991) Effects of parent involvement on change in student achievement in reading and math, in S. Silvern (ed.) *Literacy Through Family, Community, and School Interaction*, Greenwich, Conn.: Jai.

Farquhar, C., Blatchford, P., Burke, J., Plewis, I. and Tizard, B. (1985) A comparison of views of parents and reception teachers, *Education 3–13*, Vol. 2, pp. 17–22.

Feitelson, D. and Goldstein, Z. (1986) Patterns of book ownership and reading to young children in Israeli school-orientated and non school-orientated families, *Reading Teacher*, Vol. 39, pp. 924–30.

Ferreiro, E. and Teberosky, A. (1982) *Literacy before Schooling*, London: Heinemann.

Fitzgerald, J., Spiegel, D. L. and Cunningham, J. W. (1991) The relationship between parental literacy level and perceptions of emergent literacy, *Journal of Reading Behavior*, Vol. 23, no. 2, pp. 191–214.

Goelman, H., Oberg, A. and Smith, F. (eds.) (1984) *Awakening to Literacy*, Exeter, New Hampshire: Heinemann.

Goodall, M. (1984) Can four year olds 'read' words in the environment? *Reading Teacher*, Vol. 37, no. 6, pp. 478–82.

Goodman, K. (1973) Psycholinguistic universals in the reading process, in F. Smith (ed.) *Psycholinguistics and Reading*, New York: Holt, Rinehart & Winston.

Goodman, Y. (1980) The roots of literacy, *Claremont Reading Conference Yearbook*, Vol. 44, pp. 1–12.

Goodman, Y. and Altwerger, B. (1981) Print awareness in preschool children: a study of the development of literacy in preschool children. Occasional paper no. 4, Program in language and literacy, University of Arizona, September.

Goswami, U. (1990) A special link between rhyming skills and the use of orthographic analogies by beginning readers, *Journal of Child Psychology and Psychiatry*, Vol. 31, pp. 301–11.

Goswami, U. and Bryant, P. (1990) *Phonological Skills and Learning to Read*, Hove, East Sussex: Lawrence Erlbaum Associates.

Graves, D. H. (1982) *Writing: Teachers and Children at Work*, Exeter, N.H.: Heinemann.

Griffiths, A. and Hamilton, D. (1984) *Parent, Teacher, Child: Working Together in Children's Learning*, London, New York: Methuen.

Hall, N. (1987) *The Emergence of Literacy*, Sevenoaks, Kent: Hodder & Stoughton.

Hall, N. (1991) Play and the emergence of literacy, in J. F. Christie (ed.) *Play and Early Literacy Development*, Albany: State University of New York Press.

Hall, N., Herring, G., Henn, H. and Crawford, L. (1989) *Parental Views on Writing and the Teaching of Writing*, Manchester: School of Education, Manchester Polytechnic.

Hannon, P. (1987) A study of the effects of parental involvement in the teaching of reading on children's reading test performance, *British Journal of Educational Psychology*, Vol. 57, no. 1, pp. 56–72.

Hannon, P. (1990) Parental involvement in preschool literacy development, in D. Wray (ed.) *Emerging Partnerships: Current Research in Language and Literacy*, BERA Dialogues in Education, Vol. 4, Clevedon, Avon: Multilingual Matters.

Hannon, P. and Cuckle, P. (1984) Involving parents in the teaching of reading: a study of current school practice, *Educational Research*, Vol. 26, no. 1, pp. 7–13.

Hannon, P. and Jackson, A. (1987) The Belfield Reading Project final report, London and Rochdale: National Children's Bureau in association with Belfield Community Council.

Hannon, P., Jackson, A. and Weinberger, J. (1986) Parents' and teachers' strategies in hearing young children read, *Research Papers in Education*, Vol. 1, pp. 16–25.

Hannon, P. and James, S. (1990) Parents' and teachers' perspectives on preschool literacy development, *British Educational Research Journal*, Vol. 16, no. 3, pp. 259–72.

Hannon, P., Weinberger, J. and Nutbrown, C. (1991) A study of work with parents to promote early literacy development, *Research Papers in Education*, Vol. 6, no. 2, pp. 77–97.

Harste, J. C., Burke, C. L. and Woodward, V. A. (1982) Children's language and world: initial encounters with print, in J. A. Langer and M. T. Smith Burke (1982) *Reader Meets Author/Bridging the Gap*, Newark, DE: IRA.

Harste, J., Woodward, V. and Burke, C. (1984) *Language Stories and Literacy Lessons*, Portsmouth, N.H.: Heinemann.

Heath, S. B. (1983) *Ways with Words: Language, Life and Work in Communities and Classrooms*, Cambridge University Press.

Her Majesty's Inspectorate (1990) *The Teaching and Learning of Language and Literacy*, London: HMSO.

Hewison, J. and Tizard, J. (1980) Parental involvement and reading attainment, *British Journal of Educational Psychology*, Vol. 50, pp. 209–15.

Hiebert, E. H. (1978) Preschool children's understanding of written language, *Child Development*, Vol. 49, pp. 1231–4.

Hughes, M., Wikeley, F. and Nash, T. (1994) *Parents and their Children's Schools*, Oxford: Blackwell.

Inner London Education Authority (1985) *Improving Primary Schools: Report of the Committee on Primary Education*, London: ILEA.

Isenberg, J. and Jacob, E. (1983) Literacy and symbolic play: a review of the literature, *Childhood Education*, Vol. 59, no. 4, pp. 272–6.

Iverson, B. K., Brownlee, G. D. and Walberg, H. J. (1981) Parent–teacher contacts and student learning, *Journal of Educational Research*, Vol. 24, no. 6, pp. 394–6.

Kontos, S. (1986) What preschool children know about reading and how they learn it, *Young Children*, Vol. 42, no. 1, pp. 58–65.

Kroll, B. M. (1983) Antecedents of individual differences in children's writing attainment, in B. M. Kroll and C. G. Wells (eds.) *Explorations in the Development of Writing*, Chichester: Wiley.

Lamme, L. and Olmsted, P. (1977) Family reading habits and children's progress in reading. Paper presented at the annual meeting of the International Reading Association, Miami Beach, Florida, 2–6 May.

Leichter, H. J. (1974) The family as educator, *Teachers College Records*, Vol. 76, pp. 175–217, New York: Teachers College Press.

Lomax, C. M. (1979) Interest in books and stories and effects of storytelling on vocabulary, in M. M. Clark and W. M. Cheyne (eds.) (1979) *Studies in Preschool Education*, London: Hodder & Stoughton.

Maclean, M., Bryant, P. and Bradley, L. (1987) Rhymes, nursery rhymes and reading in early childhood, *Merrill-Palmer Quarterly*, Vol. 33, no. 3, pp. 255–81.

Mason, J. M. (1992) Reading stories to pre-literate children: a proposed connection to reading, in P. B. Gough, L. C. Ehri and R. Treiman (eds.) *Reading Acquisition*, London: Laurence Erlbaum.

Masonheimer, P., Drum, P. and Ehri, L. (1984) Does environmental print identification lead children into word reading? *Journal of Reading Behaviour*, Vol. 16, pp. 257–71.

Meek, M. (1982) *Learning to Read*, London: Bodley Head.

Meek, M. (1988) *How Texts Teach What Readers Learn*, Stroud, Glos.: Thimble Press.

Meyer, L. A., Hastings, C. N. and Linn, R. L. (1990) *Home Support for Emerging Literacy: What Parents Do that Correlates with Early Reading Achievement.* Technical Report No. 518, Cambridge, Mass: Illinois Unit, Urbana: Centre for the Study of Reading.

Millard, E. (1994) *Developing Readers in the Middle Years*, Buckinghamshire: Open University Press.

Minns, H. (1990) *Read It to Me Now*, London: Virago Education with the University of London Institute of Education.

Moon, C. (1980) *Individualised Reading*, Reading: Centre for the Teaching of Reading, University of Reading.

Moon, C. and Wells, G. (1979) The influence of home on learning to read, *Journal of Research in Reading*, Vol. 2, no. 1, pp. 53–62.

Morrow, L. (1983) Home and school correlates of early interest in literature, *Journal of Educational Research*, Vol. 76, pp. 221–30.

Moss, E. (1977) What is a good book? The peppermint lesson, in M. Meek, A. Warlow and G. Barton (eds.) *The Cool Web: the Pattern of Children's Reading*, London: Bodley Head.

Muehl, S. and Dinello, M. C. (1976) Early first-grade skills related to subsequent reading performance: a seven-year follow-up study, *Journal of Reading Behaviour*, Vol. 8, pp. 67–81.

Nebor, J. N. (1986) *Parental Influence and Involvement on Reading Achievement*, U.S. Illinois, information analyses, ED 286150.

Newson, J. and Newson, E. (1976) *Seven Years Old in the Home Environment*, Harmondsworth, Middlesex: Penguin.

Newson, J. and Newson, E., with Barnes, P. (1977) *Perspectives on School at Seven Years Old*, London: Allen & Unwin.

Ninio, A. and Bruner, J. (1978) The achievements and antecedents of labelling, *Journal of Child Language*, Vol. 5, pp. 5–15.

Nutbrown, C., Hannon, P. and Weinberger, J. (1991) Training teachers to work with parents to promote early literacy development, *International Journal of Early Childhood*, Vol. 23, no. 2, pp. 1–10.

Ormerod, J. (1992) The inevitability of transformation: designing picture books for children and adults, in M. Styles, E. Bearne and V. Watson (eds.) *After Alice: Exploring Children's Literature*, London: Cassell.

Payton, S. (1984) Developing awareness of print: a young child's first steps towards literacy. *Educational Review*, occasional publications no. 2, University of Birmingham.

Pellegrini, A. D., Galda, L., Dresden, J. and Cox, S. (1991) A longitudinal study of the predictive relations among symbolic play, linguistic verbs, and early literacy, *Research in the Teaching of English*, Vol. 25, no. 2, pp. 219–35.

Read, C. (1971) Preschool children's knowledge of English phonology, *Harvard Educational Review*, Vol. 4, pp. 1–34.

Robinson, F. and Sulzby, E. (1984) Parents and children and 'favourite' books: an interview study, in J. A. Niles and L. A. Harris (eds.) *Changing Perspectives on Research in Reading and Language Processing Instruction*, 33rd Yearbook of the National Reading Conference.

Rossman, J. F. (1975) Remedial readers: did parents read to them at home? *Journal of Reading*, Vol. 17, pp. 622–5.

Schickedanz, J. (1990) *Adam's Righting Revolutions: One Child's Literacy Development from Infancy through Grade One*, Portsmouth, N.H.: Heinemann.

Schieffelin, B. B. and Gilmore, P. (eds.) (1986) *Acquisition of Literacy: Ethnographic Perspectives*, Norwood, N.J.: Ablex.

School Examinations and Assessment Council (1991,1992) *Standard Assessment Tasks*, London, HMSO.

Scollon, R. and Scollon, S. B. K. (1981) *Narrative, Literacy and Face in Interethnic Communication*, Norwood, N.J.: Ablex.

Share, D. L., Jorm, A. R., Maclean, R. and Matthews, R. (1984) Sources of individual differences in reading acquisition, *Journal of Educational Psychology*, Vol. 76, pp. 1309–24.

Sheldon, W. D. and Carrillo, L. W. (1952) Relation of parents, home, and certain developmental characteristics to children's reading ability, *Elementary School Journal*, Vol. 5, pp. 262–70.

Smith, F. (1978) *Reading*, Cambridge University Press.

Smith, F. (1982) *Writing and the Writer*, London: Heinemann Educational.

Snow, C., Nathan, D. and Perlmann, R. (1985) Assessing children's knowledge about bookreading, in L. Galda and A. Pellegrini (eds.) *Play, Language, and Stories*, Norwood, N.J.: Ablex.

Snow, C. E., and Ninio, A. (1986) The contracts of literacy: what children learn from learning to read books, in W. H. Teale and E. Sulzby (eds.) (1986) *Emergent Literacy*, Norwood, N.J.: Ablex.

Snow, C. E., Barnes, W. S., Chandler, J., Goodman, I. F. and Hemphill, L. (1991) *Unfulfilled Expectations: Home and School Influences on Literacy*, London: Harvard University Press.

Steedman, C. (1982) *The Tidy House: Little Girls Writing*, London: Virago.

Street, B. (1984) *Literacy in Theory and Practice*, Cambridge University Press.

Styles, M., Bearne, E. and Watson, V. (1992) *After Alice: Exploring Children's Literature*, London, Cassell.

Sulzby, E. (1985) Children's emergent reading of favourite storybooks: a developmental study, *Reading Research Quarterly*, Vol. 20, pp. 458–81.

Sulzby, E. and Teale, W. H. (1987) *Young children's storybook reading: longitudinal study of parent–child interaction and children's independent functioning*. Final report to the Spencer Foundation, Ann Arbor: University of Michigan.

Sutton, M. H. (1964) Readiness for reading at the kindergarten level, *Reading Teacher*, Vol. 17, pp. 234–40.

Taylor, D. (1981) The family and the development of reading skills and values, *Journal of Research in Reading*, Vol. 4, no. 2, pp. 92–103.

Taylor, D. (1983) *Family Literacy: Young Children Learning to Read and Write*, London: Heinemann Educational.

Taylor, D. and Dorsey-Gaines, C. (1988) *Growing Up Literate: Learning from Inner-City Families*, Portsmouth, N.H.: Heinemann.

Teale, W. H. (1978) Positive environments for learning to read: what studies of early readers tell us, *Language Arts*, Vol. 55, no. 8, pp. 922–32.

Teale, W. H. (1981) Parents reading to their children: what we know and need to know, *Language Arts*, Vol. 58, pp. 902–12.

Teale, W. H. and Sulzby, E. (eds.) (1986) *Emergent Literacy: Writing and Reading*, Norwood, N.J.: Ablex.

Tizard, B. and Hughes, M. (1984) *Young Children Learning: Talking and Thinking at Home and at School*, London: Fontana.

Tizard, B., Mortimore, J. and Burchell, B. (1981) *Involving Parents in Nursery and Infant Schools*, London: Grant McIntyre.

Tizard, J., Schofield, W. N. and Hewison, J. (1982) Collaboration between teachers and parents in assisting children's reading, *British Journal of Educational Psychology*, Vol. 52, pp. 1–15.

Tizard, B., Blatchford, P., Burke, J., Farquhar, C. and Plewis, I. (1988) *Young Children at School in the Inner City*. Hove and London: Lawrence Erlbaum Associates.

Toomey, D. M. (1989) How home–school relations policies can increase educational inequality, *Australian Journal of Education*, Vol. 33, no. 3, pp. 284–98.

Topping, K. and Wolfendale, S. (eds.) (1985) *Parental Involvement in Children's Reading*, London: Croom Helm.

Tucker, N. (1993) The 'good book': literacy and developmental aspects, in R. Beard (ed.) *Teaching Literacy: Balancing Perspectives*, Sevenoaks, Kent: Hodder & Stoughton.

Vygotsky, L. S. (1962) *Thought and Language*, Cambridge: MIT Press and Wiley.

Vygotsky, L. S. (1978) *Mind in Society*, Cambridge, MA: Harvard University Press.

Wade, B. (1984) Story at home and school. *Educational Review*, occasional publication no. 10, University of Birmingham.

Wade, B. (1990) Approaches to reading, in B. Wade (ed.) *Reading for Real*, Milton Keynes: Open University Press.

Walker, G. H., and Kuerbitz, I. E. (1979) Reading to preschoolers as an aid to successful beginning reading, *Reading Improvement*, Vol. 16, pp. 149–54.

Watson, V. (1992) Irresponsible writers and responsible readers, in M. Styles, E. Bearne and V. Watson (eds.) *After Alice: Exploring Children's Literature*, London: Cassell.

Wechsler, D. (1967) *WPPSI Manual (Wechsler Preschool and Primary Scale of Intelligence)*, New York: The Psychological Corporation.

Weinberger, J. (1983) *The Fox Hill Reading Workshop*, London: Family Service Units.

Weinberger, J. (1988) Reading: parents and preschool, *Reading*, Vol. 22, no. 3, pp. 164–7.

Weinberger, J. (1993) A longitudinal study of literacy experiences, the role of parents, and children's literacy development. University of Sheffield: unpublished PhD thesis.

Weinberger, J., Jackson, A. and Hannon, P. (1986) Variation in take-up of a project to involve parents in the teaching of reading, *Educational Studies*, Vol. 12, pp. 159–74.

Wells, G. (1985a) *Language, Learning and Education*, Windsor: NFER, Nelson.

Wells, G. (1985b) Pre-school literacy-related activities and success in school, in D. R. Olson, N. Torrance and A. Hildyard (eds.) *Literacy, Language and Learning*, Cambridge University Press.

Wells, G. (1987) *The Meaning Makers: Children Learning Language and Using Language to Learn*, London: Hodder & Stoughton.

White, J. (1990) On literacy and gender, in R. Carter (ed.) *Knowledge About Language and the Curriculum*, London: Hodder & Stoughton.

Young, D. (1989) *Manual for the Group Reading Test* (3rd edn), Sevenoaks: Hodder & Stoughton.

Zifcak, M. (1981) Phonological awareness and reading acquisition, *Contemporary Educational Psychology*, Vol. 6, pp. 117–26.

Children's books mentioned

Ahlberg, J. and Ahlberg, A. (1986) *The Jolly Postman*, London: Heinemann.

Briggs, R. (1978) *The Snowman*, Harmondsworth: Picture Puffins.

Carle, E. (1974) *The Very Hungry Caterpillar*, Harmondsworth: Puffin Books.

Dahl, R. (1980) *The Twits*, Harmondsworth: Puffin Books.

Grant, J. (1983) *A Trap for He-Man*, Loughborough: Ladybird.

Grant, J. (1984) *Castle Greyskull under Attack!* Loughborough: Ladybird Books.

Hill, E. (1983) *Where's Spot?* Harmondsworth: Picture Puffins.

Hunia, F. (1977) *Three Little Pigs*, Loughborough: Ladybird Books.

Hutchins, P. (1971) *Titch*, Harmondsworth: Picture Puffins.

Kerr, J. (1973) *The Tiger who Came to Tea*, London: Collins, Picture Lions.

King-Smith, D. (1988) *Sophie's Snail*, London: Walker Books.

King-Smith, D. (1991) *Sophie's Tom*, London: Walker Books.

Maris, R. (1988) *I Wish I Could Fly*, Harmondsworth: Picture Puffins.

McCullagh, S. (1969: 18th impression, 1992) *Roger Red-hat. One, two, three and away, introductory book A*, Glasgow: Collins Educational.

Murphy, J. (1974) *The Worst Witch*, Harmondsworth: Puffin Books.

Murphy, J. (1986) *Five Minutes Peace*, London: Walker Books.

Murray, W. (1964) *We Have Fun*, Loughborough: Ladybird Books.

Williams, V. M. (1965) *Gobbolino, the Witch's Cat*, Harmondsworth: Puffin Books.

Author index

162   *Literacy Goes to School*

Hutchins, P. 46

Isenberg, J. 37
Iverson, B. 26, 110

Jackson, A. 24
Jackson, J. 38
Jacob, E. 37
James, S. 25, 136

Kerr, J. 46
King-Smith, D. 79, 80
Kontos, S. 37
Kroll, B. 36
Kuerbitz, I. 34

Leichter, H. 20

Maclean, M. 6, 34
Maris, R. 85
Mason, J. 35
Masonheimer, P. 37
McCullagh, S. 80
Meek, M. 6, 10, 51
Millard, E. 79
Minns, H. 17, 26
Moon, C. 28, 148
Morrow, L. 9, 12
Moss, E. 125
Muehl, S. 32
Murphy, J. 46, 79
Murray, W. 49, 82

Nash, T. 26
Nebor, J. 12
Newson, E. 18, 22, 136
Newson, J. 18, 22, 136
Ninio, A. 9, 47
Nutbrown, C. 49, 136

Ormerod, J. 7

Payton, S. 5, 20
Pellegrini, A. 37

Pidgeon, S. 7

Read, C. 10
Robinson, F. 49
Rossman, J. 35

Schickedanz, J. 11
S.E.A.C. 148
Scollon, R. 9
Scollon, S. 9
Share, D. 34
Smith, F. 6, 14
Snow, C. 9, 26, 29, 36, 110
Spiegel, D. 19
Steedman, C. 48
Street, B. 13
Styles, M. 7
Sulzby, E. 9, 49
Sutton, M. 35

Taylor, D. 4, 15, 16, 17, 21
Teale, W. 9, 17, 31
Teberosky, A. 6, 11
Tizard, B. 13, 25, 29, 38, 48
Tizard, J. 23, 36, 37, 38, 105, 151
Toomey, D. 25, 136
Topping, K. 24
Tucker, N. 125

Vygotsky, L. 12, 21, 37, 84

Wade, B. 7, 35
Walker, G. 34
Watson, V. 129
Wechsler, D. 150
Weinberger, J. 24, 49, 136, 148
Wells, G. 7, 8, 9, 12, 13, 28, 29, 34, 46
White, J. 79
Wikeley, F. 26
Wolfendale, S. 24
Woodward, V. 4, 10, 18

Young, D. 148, 151

Subject index